Bishop Kim W. Brown, DMin
presents

Boiling

Our Children

*A Kingdom Parenting Approach
To Healing Generations and Transforming Legacies*

Spirit Filled Creations

BOILING OUR CHILDREN
A Kingdom Parenting Approach to Healing Generations and Transforming Legacies

Copyright © 2024 Kim W. Brown

Published by Spirit Filled Creations LLC
Chesapeake, Virginia 23323
www.SpiritFilledCreations.com
Email: SpiritFilledCreations7@gmail.com

This book or parts thereof may not be reproduced in any form, stored in a retrieval system, or transmitted in any form by any means – electronic, mechanical, photocopy, recording, or otherwise – without prior written permission of the publisher and authors, except as provided by United States of America copyright law.

Unless otherwise indicated, scriptures marked KJV are taken from the KING JAMES VERSION (KJV), public domain. Scriptures marked TM are taken from the THE MESSAGE: THE BIBLE IN CONTEMPORARY ENGLISH (TM): Scripture taken from THE MESSAGE: THE BIBLE IN CONTEMPORARY ENGLISH, copyright©1993, 1994, 1995, 1996, 2000, 2001, 2002. Used by permission of NavPress Publishing Group. Scripture quotations marked TPT are from The Passion Translation®. Copyright © 2017, 2018, 2020 by Passion & Fire Ministries, Inc. Used by permission. All rights reserved. ThePassionTranslation.com.

All rights reserved.

Cover Design: Spirit Filled Creations

International Standard Book Number: 979-8-9898109-0-1

First Edition

Printed in the United States of America

*This book is dedicated to my grandchildren,
James, Jaxon, Kennedy, and Kaylyn.
Each of you will make the Lord's name great in the earth
and leave marks that will never be erased.
I pray that your Grandchildren are blessed because of the
inheritance of Faith Mom-Mom and Pop-Pop leave you.*

Thank you!

The danger of expressing gratitude is found in leaving someone out. This work has been delayed and detoured. But I realize it was God's hand putting the motivation and team together to manifest His desires for such a time as this. Thank God for the ability to process and declare years of lessons and truths so other parents will not have the learning curve that I did. My life partner, lover, and friend, Valerie, has the queenly ability to be a pusher without shoving; your patience with me is amazing.

My children, James, Keshia, Kimberly, and Linwood have made people think that I actually know what I am doing and that I have something worth listening to. Thank you for being the inspiration to share. Your success is evidence of God's grace, not my ability.

Deaconess Monique Anderson. You are a gift to the Kingdom! Many books would still be in the hearts of people and not on shelves if it were not for you. Thank you for the looks on Sundays that convicted me to continue to write.

Finally, to the best, and I mean best with conviction, church family and church staff anywhere. Your patience, commitment, and Love have enabled me to write this offering to families in the present and the future. May God continue to use each of us to **CHANGE LIVES**!

Table of Contents

Foreword 9

Introduction 13

The Purpose Of The Family 19

Children And Faith 27

Children And Destiny 31

Children And God 43

Children And Decision-Making 53

Children: Finances And Work 59

Children And Money 71

Children And Education 83

Children: Family And Discipline 95

Children And Divorce 103

Children And Relationships 113

Children And Death 123

Children: Authority And Fellowship 129

Children And Community 135

Under New Management 141

The Choice Is Yours 147

A Final Prayer 159

"Parenting is not about perfecting, but about persisting with love, guidance, and the unwavering commitment to nurture the unique potential within each child."

-Anonymous

Foreword

It is hard to read a headline that does not refer to a shooting in our community on any given day. Our children are dying, the divorce rate is beyond reason, crime is at an all-time high, and it appears as if people's anger is insurmountable. I believe the social ills of our society can be traced back to one primary root cause: the breakdown of the nuclear family consisting of a two-parent (dad and mom) household. This destruction has led to the manifestation of single-parent homes, which has impacted the development of our children and future generations. As I write these words, I desire they become the foundation and launching pad for the healing of a generation in saving our future.

Writing this book was confirmed on Christmas day. My family (Valerie, James, Kimberly, and Keshia) were all together in the family room preparing to open gifts. Christmas morning has always been a time of prayer and thanksgiving in our home. This particular morning would prove to be life-changing and like no other before. As the family determined it to be my turn to open presents, I noticed their anticipation transcended into a moment of inspiration. My son James handed me his gift. I can still remember how special I felt. I was requested to read the card he selected aloud. Hearing words like role model, character, and integrity were amazing. My son, who is usually reserved, appeared excited about what the card said to me. Upon completing the reading, he hands me a gift. While unwrapping, I noticed the eyes of my family expanding under the pressure of tears. While the card was touching, I remember wondering why there were tears. It was not until I had opened my gift that I understood. James was my wife Valerie's son from a former marriage. Observing our family, no one would have ever known that James was not my biological son. I had been in his life since he was two years old and had raised him as my own. We all have wow times when we are overwhelmed beyond our wildest expectations. This was indeed one of those moments for me. My son presented me with legal documentation acknowledging that he had changed his last name to match mine. James Bright was now James Brown. That moment confirmed that I had something to share with the nations about raising children. It is with that spirit that I hope the words, wisdom, and anointing upon these pages will be an eternal offering to God and a tremendous blessing to all who share.

    The Bible's first book, Genesis, reminds us that the family was not only created but is also the foundation of our society. Before the church is established in Acts, the family is formed before any scriptures on giving or ministry. If the foundation is weak, then the building cannot be established. The first learning setting is the home. Most of what we become and believe is shaped by the home's environment. Parents are the original role models. We now live in a prescription-driven, Ritalin-giving society that has forgotten our first responsibility as defined by the Word of God. The family is the bedrock of our society. We must commit to returning to the principles of morality and conviction that brought us. As we digest and explore the pages of this parental offering, I pray that every Father and Mother will find renewed strength and a sacred conviction to be a present and effective source of inspiration and direction for future generations.

A Kingdom Parenting Approach
to Healing Generations and Transforming Legacies

"Your children are the greatest gift God will give to you, and their souls the heaviest responsibility He will place in your hands. Take time with them, teach them to have faith in God. Be a person in whom they can have faith."

- Lisa Wingate

Introduction

It is Wednesday evening, and I am driving home from returning my daughter to school for her fall semester of study. I know you are wondering what this has to do with the needed insight into raising our children. The fact that I pastor Mount Lebanon Baptist Church and it is a Wednesday should give you a clue; it's Bible study and mid-week worship time. However, one of the staff ministers will serve the congregation's spiritual needs tonight. It was more important for me to share with my daughter in another rite of passage. This is her second semester in college. Someone once said that to succeed at anything, you must determine what you will fail at. My wife and I decided long ago that we would succeed as parents. At times, that requires me to fail at ministering. I remind myself that I only get one chance at being a father, and many moments are once-in-a-lifetime opportunities.

I am a PK (preacher's kid), and although my mother and father truly loved me, I still remember feeling that church was more important than I was as a child. I am the product of divorce. Even as an adult with grown children, I still feel the pain of my childhood. Through this book, I desire that my experience will be an opportunity for the Lord to prevent my pain from manifesting in the lives of other young people.

Much has been written about raising children. During these critical times, we need a voice of the Kingdom to refocus us with Biblical principles and paradigms, and I believe I am one of those vital and credible voices.

Parenting today is even more strenuous and stressful. Careers, soccer practices, sociological stresses, the pressures of social media, and the rat race of chasing the American dream have forced many of our young to be parented by Wii, Nintendo, PlayStation, YouTube, TikTok, and Instagram. What will happen if we do not arrest our morals and re-establish family values. In that case, we will continue to mis-steward their lives and provide greater opportunities for the erosion of our society. One of the greatest blessings and responsibilities given to man by God is training the next generation.

My lovely wife Valerie and I are blessed with two children and have been led by God to become surrogate parents to many others. I bring to this oracle over three decades of parenting and learning many lessons. When we fix the role of parents and the relationship with children, we will immediately see the fruit of increase in our families and communities.

When I was a child, you worked in the yard, took out the trash, said "yes ma'am" and "no sir," and greatly respected all adults. It can be said that every generation becomes more relaxed in its moral standards and core values. Please let me sound the alarm before it is too late to turn our society around. "We are boiling our children."

In 2 Kings chapter 6, a story is recorded involving two women. In the story, the women find themselves amid a famine and are confronted with making decisions about economic survival. The two women decide to survive by eating their sons. The story says that they boil the first woman's son. It has always amazed me how the Bible can be thousands of years old and still be as relevant as it was written yesterday. This story speaks clearly to our current sociological concerns about raising our children. Several similar conclusions can be drawn. First, the women are concerned with surviving during the famine.

One of the most complicated problems confronting parents today is surviving during critically desperate economic times. Parents are faced with making decisions based on financial dynamics daily. In fact, parents have pawned their children's futures by living beyond their economic means. Keeping up with the Jones has caused us to drive, wear, and live in more than we can afford. To make ends meet, many parents work overtime and multiple jobs, which prevents them from having quality time with family.

Secondly, the women make a covenant with each other rather than with God. We live such a fast-paced, multi-tasking life that there is often no time for God or spirituality. Many parents have more defined relationships with fraternal organizations and sororities, booster clubs, and workout facilities than with the Kingdom. While it is important to seek people's advice, there is no greater advisor than the Holy Spirit.

Finally, they boil their sons. The very theme of this book is rooted in this part of the story. Subjecting something to heat, such as boiling, alters its molecular composition, causing it to soften. Notice the story does not say they baked or fried their sons but boiled them. I suggest we are boiling our children just like the women in the biblical narrative.

Our children appear to have unusual anger problems like never before because we are heating them. We have a generation with challenges in controlling their anger in the mildest environments and have been diagnosed with ADHD (better known as attention deficit). Hold on, stop right there; I am not downplaying the medical experts and the reality of attention disorders. However, I do believe many are misdiagnosed. Proper discipline and structure could be the answer for those who are medicated. Lastly, adolescents have difficulty working, remaining committed, and accomplishing goals. They are soft. Simply as a point of reference, I was required to work during my summers through high school and my undergraduate college program. Could it be that by allowing our young people to sleep in late on the weekend, avoid responsibilities and chores, and work overtime to pay for their expensive lifestyles, we are indeed boiling our children? This theory does demand our attention and observation. Join me as we explore raising a generation of soft children because parents have substituted quality influence and parental responsibility with materialism and a lack of parental attention and support. Hopefully, along this journey, we will save our children and release them into a greater destiny, reminding those called to the parental ministry to refocus and reprioritize their lives. I hear a generation of children thanking us for training them in the way they should go.

A Kingdom Parenting Approach
to Healing Generations and Transforming Legacies

The Purpose Of The Family

Have you ever considered what God desired to accomplish when He created the Family? The eleventh chapter of Numbers describes a situation that establishes a framework for perhaps understanding the family concept. This story illustrates the daughters of Zelophehad petitioning Moses for their father's inheritance. Inheritance is much more than money. The inheritance of a family is the stability of developing and understanding our God-given purpose in life. The erosion of it in our society is the most significant detriment to the convictions and character of our communities. This loss has caused a grave compromise in our standards and beliefs.

The statistics of our present day are seriously frightening. Twenty-five percent of 15-year-old females and thirty percent of 15-year-old males are sexually active. In comparison, 18-year-old females are sixty-six percent sexually active and sixty-eight percent of 18-year-old males. A single mother heads eighty percent of single-parent households in America. That means 1 in 5 children under 18, about 15.7 million, are raised without a father. When I examined the story in Numbers 27:1-11, I discovered what I believe the overall purpose of the family was: to exemplify how God intends for the family to operate and develop generations.

Foremost, in the mind of God, was to develop a vehicle for Generational Training. The family is the University for training future generations. In verse three, the daughters state that their father was not among the followers who rebelled against the Lord. Essentially, they are communicating that they saw their daddy display behavior shaping their belief system. The initial purpose of family is education. Parents are the most important educators a child will ever have. We teach both intentionally and vicariously. Everything that our children observe is a lesson. What we say, what we do, and who we spend time with are all classes in the University of Life that they learn from. This training should include four pillars of family training: beliefs, identity, character, and purpose. The family is the vehicle that God created to make sure the beliefs of our faith are communicated, modeled, and taught to the next generation.

When we are born, we are given two names. Perhaps the most important name is our last name, our sir name. This name gives us our identity. The Bible teaches us that a good name is more valuable than gold. I remember speaking with one of our Elder's sons when he was a young boy, and the conversation was about stealing. He told me his dad had taught him that a Richards does not lie, steal, or cheat. His father had instilled in him an identity based on his name. Parents, please be careful to provide a good name while providing sneakers, clothes, cars, and other material things. This is a great place to pause and ask, "What does your name stand for? What reputation does your name inspire in the community? Is your name a standard bearer?"

Our name also transfers character and purpose. Just as the Levites had a generational purpose, I believe the family should be a training ground for the same. I am proud that all my children are in ministry. While I never forced them to be, it was made clear that our family serves the people of God. From an early age, they were led to be engaged in serving in the church and community. They have non-profits that enable them to serve.

Another purpose of the family is to provide an opportunity for generational transfer. It is so sad when people die after working all their lives, and all they can leave for the next generation is a mortgaged home and an old automobile. Again, in Numbers 27:7, the daughter of Zelophehad is given the inheritance of their father. The Bible teaches that someone who does not leave an inheritance is worse than an infidel. I believe we are called to leave an inheritance that includes two things. Wealth and wisdom are the inheritance we should work to leave the next generation as an inheritance. One of the simplest ways to leave an inheritance of wealth is through life insurance. We are driving and wearing our children's inheritance. Please know I have no problem with people living very well. This is not a declaration of envy for those who live a prosperous life. But I cannot tell you how many times I have seen a GoFundMe campaign for someone driving a 7 series BMW, living in a five-bedroom home, who did not have life insurance. I have some alarming news to share with you: everyone will die! Now that I have gotten that shocking news out of the way, please stop, call, and inquire about life insurance. The old statement that "every generation has to work for theirs" is a false narrative of what we should accomplish. One of the reasons why the wealth gap continues to expand in America is because the wealthy leave the next generation an inheritance that empowers them to achieve more and go further. If your children are young, establish a trust, provide a capable estate executive to oversee, and provide a trustee to ensure your children steward the wealth you leave. Suppose you know that your children are maturing slowly. In that case, you can set up a trust with benchmarks of maturity written into it, so their future is provided for as they display a maturity that equips them to handle the inheritance. But we must begin to transfer generational wealth and wisdom to secure the future of unborn generations.

I believe an unspoken purpose of the family is generational transformation. Before the daughters of Zelophehad received their inheritance, it had only been given to the sons of a father. They break the pattern of society by requesting it, and they make it clear that there are no sons. Their ask causes Moses to rewrite the rules of inheritance. Afterward, the daughters could receive their father's inheritance. What a transformation! They changed how the community operated. I believe the purpose of a family is to create and cultivate community change. What in your community is better because of your family? What is different because your family exists? What are the problems your family is addressing? How will generations to come be better because of your bloodline? The family should birth change agents, problem solvers, and destiny deliverers. Teach and empower your children to have a sociological impact. Their school should be better because they attend. Their class should be better because they are a student with impact. From an early age, we are responsible for ensuring our children know that wherever they go, they should leave footprints and fingerprints that communicate they came that way. What they do and where they go should leave a lasting impact on those who follow. We should be raising leaders, not followers. I know you are thinking, as you read, that everyone is not a leader. I disagree; if we train our children to lead and remind them of their greatness, they will become leaders.

How can I make such a definitive statement, you ask. Because the Bible teaches us that we are the "head," not the "tail." I believe every child can be an agent of transformation. If only we would model, inspire, and celebrate it.

Finally, the purpose of the family is to provide a generational testimony. When the time has expired and your family no longer exists, will your name be recorded and remembered? I am excited that, at the time of this writing, our local hospital is building a new chapel. The chapel will be named in honor of the work that my wife Valerie and I have accomplished in our community. When I am no longer breathing, a testimony will be established, making a legacy mark that speaks of our family's work in ministry. The daughters of Zelophehad ask a question, "Why should our father's name disappear?" How sad it would be to leave a disappearing name on the earth. The family becomes the provider of the legacy of mention. It is not just our name that we should be working to keep visible, but our heavenly father's name as well. What has your family done to ensure the heavenly Father's name does not disappear? As the patriarch of my family, I desire that when I am long gone, my great-grandchildren will still be. As I write, I receive pictures of my grandson's first day of school. I desire that he understands that when he is grown, our family will always make sure that the name of Christ is known on the earth. We represent Christ. We teach Christ. We model the life of Christ. The family is the institution responsible for teaching the love of Christ to the next generation. Unfortunately, far too often, the family has become the leading teacher of bigotry, hatred, and indifference. If we are not careful, the name of our father will soon disappear. Mom and Dad, it is up to you. Know that you understand the real purpose of a family and make today a starting point of change: training, transfer, transformation, and testimony. You can and have the opportunity to create a lasting legacy of hope. The family, your family, is the instrument that God desires to use to accomplish it.

Children And Faith

The key to understanding the responsibility of parenting is to recognize it as a God-given and God-called ministry. God ordains life. And when we are allowed to steward the journey of another human being, we must understand it as a kingdom assignment. Children represent the heritage of our bloodline, the legacy of our life on earth. Parenting is too important to be entered into without proper thought and training. As such, you are your child's first pastor, first teacher, and most impactful role model.

In his book *It Starts At Home*, Kurt Bruner suggests two windows of opportunity for training children. The imprint period is from birth to seven years old, and the impression period is seven to fifteen. According to Bruner, at sixteen, parents move into a third level of the relationship with their children, in which they become coaches.

In the sixth chapter of Deuteronomy, God instructs parents and family leaders with several principles to help steward the responsibility. One of the most remarkable ways in which we learn is through repetition. Specifically, in verse seven, God tells parents to repeat God's commands again and again. When our children were teenagers, every time they left the house to go to a party or a football game or just drove to the store, they knew they would be stopped at the door, and the same words would be repeated. I can still hear our children as they stopped and said, "Do we have to get the speech again." God tells them to talk about them at home, on a journey, when lying down, and when getting up. I call this parental insulation. Reminding our children what the standard for the family has to become a part of our everyday lifestyle. There is no substitute for talking to them; never forget that the world is. Media, music, friends, and associates speak carnality all day. Parents must have a strong voice to combat those voices.

Later in the same chapter of Deuteronomy six, God tells the parents to wear them (commands) on their foreheads and tie them to their wrists. I refer to this concept as parental inspection. As parents, we must intentionally throw ourselves into our children's world. Know their friends. Share in their social conversations.

While I believe in respecting personal space, we must never forget that it is the parent's responsibility to supervise and steward the growth of young people. Our children were never allowed to secure their bedroom doors without our acknowledgment. Our children also knew that we would explore all areas of their room at a moment's notice. I just heard some liberal-minded parent get nervous because they feel that their child's privacy will be forever breached by the concept I am suggesting. Parents are responsible for the home and the children. Never allow the adversary to make you feel guilty for accepting the full responsibility to inspect your children's hands. Look for gang beads and other items that can give insight into the mind and movement of your child and prevent them from going contrary to their destiny before it is too late.

Too many times, young people are not clear on the expectations that parents have for them. In verse nine of Deuteronomy chapter 6, God instructs the parents to write the commands on the doorpost of your house and your gates. This image helps us to understand how to communicate parental instructions. Often, parents communicate expectations without confirming that the child fully understands. The doorpost was a public expression of the commands of God. Parents are responsible for living by the same standards they communicate. Parents cannot lie while teaching a standard that does not embrace lying. Parents must display the same moral convictions they are attempting to teach.

I have found that children are much better followers than listeners. Some teach children to do what they say rather than to do what they see. God tells the parents to write the commands on their foreheads. In other words, be a visible witness for your children to follow. Show your children what your values are through actions. Don't drop the children off at church for youth moments; let them see you developing your faith and serving the Kingdom. We are the greatest portrait our children have. Show them who you desire them to become. Parents should ask themselves, "If my children become what I display, what kind of adults will they be?"

Children And Destiny

Helping our offspring reach their God-given potential and destiny is perhaps one of a parent's most difficult tasks. It becomes difficult to assist our young in achieving their potential and destiny because many parents have yet to reach their own. We are confronted with a generation that decides destiny based on possible compensation and lifestyle. Ask the average person who or what they want to be in life, and they will usually answer based on how much money they think they will make.

The Bible reminds parents that children are like arrows in the hands of a mighty man (Psalm 127:3-5). If children are arrows, then parents are archers. When I first understood this metaphor, I was determined to study and understand its art form. We can learn much about raising children by studying archery. Arrows, by design, are weapons. Fathers must begin to look at their children as weapons given to them by the grace of God to impact, wound, and destroy the Kingdom of the adversary. As a parent, my greatest weapon is my children. Just as I had to learn how to use my handgun, which is a weapon, we must be trained to parent our children as such. I understand why kids have become increasingly more violent in our society; they are weapons, and they have a call upon them for warfare. Therefore, arrows must always be properly guarded because, left to themselves, they can be dangerous. It would be helpful as parents to identify several dynamics of archery that can be applied to parental responsibility. First, arrows must be aimed. What a simple but profound perspective. My wife and I have two biological children and have been guardians for several other children during our years of marriage. One lesson we have learned has been profoundly clear: each child is different. Our two biological children present different personalities. One is very laid back, and one is quite emotional. Kimberly is great with numbers, and people and very disciplined in her studies and pursuit of goals. James is lighthearted, relationally faithful, and an individual thinker. While both are arrows in my hand, they are dissimilar. While I believe in allowing children to develop their personalities and individuality, I also believe they must be aimed. Arrows do not decide the target; the archer does. As guardians, we must point out and assist them in discovering their destiny. Please allow me to share that aiming them does not mean we force them into a destiny that we choose. It means we make them aware of their obvious gifts and abilities. We have attempted to point our children toward their future based on their personalities, capabilities, and desires. Kimberly is very disciplined, good in math, and a great student; we are pointing her toward a career in accounting like her mother. James is very self-confident and determined in his thinking process and is excellent with all kinds of people. We have pointed him toward the Ministry of Helps. He has completed seminary and is currently pastoring. They are arrows. They need a target, direction, and aim. We must present opportunities and develop an atmosphere of exposure that enables our children to find their gifts and abilities while confirming a path of destiny. My son James was originally enrolled in our local fireman's academy. While attending a family conference and witnessing other young people assisting their parents in ministry, he was led to withdraw from the academy and enroll in seminary. The atmosphere of exposure pushed him into a career path that lined up with his gifts, abilities, and call.

Also, because children are arrows, they will only go as far as they are stretched. Arrows are placed in a bow, and the bow string is pulled and stretched to release the arrow. Several points can be made in relation to stretching the bow. First, a child is to be released. Arrows are not meant to stay in the quiver. The archer finds peace in releasing the arrow. We have always attempted to make our children independent. From the time a child is born, the parents are responsible for training them for deployment. The home is not the permanent place but the preparation place. Numerous parents cripple their children by not preparing them to be released properly. My wife and I are training them to grow with their responsibilities. All of our children decided to go away to school. They have already been equipped and taught that after college, they are not supposed to be living in our home. Many parents have developed a co-dependent next generation where children are unprepared for life and have difficulty being released from the home. Arrows must be released to be effective. They never achieve their purpose by staying with the archer. Secondly, while the stretching can be difficult, the arrow will only travel a distance directly with the amount of stretching that has taken place. Stretching takes hands-on participation on the part of the archer. There is no substitute for parental involvement in the life of a child. Before deciding to have children, we must be honest about the requirements and investment of time that parenting requires. Children need parents to push them. Recently, my wife observed an Asian sister pushing her child to read. The child was required to read daily and only allowed to watch one hour of television a day. The parent must know each child well enough to know how far they can be stretched. My wife and I have always been a part of our children's stretching process. They were not allowed to choose their classes in middle and high school. While they would have loved to take classes that did not fully challenge them, they needed to be stretched. As parents, we must push children to excellence in everything they do and never allow them to settle. We cannot allow them to become complacent and comfortable. They will never know what they can achieve unless they are pushed. Drive them to the difficult classes and inspire them to exceed their last accomplishment. Set goals for them and establish boundaries that allow them to reach those goals. Although every child is different, one thing remains a constant: they must be stretched. A successful child is one who has been pushed to exceed societal norms and expectations.

Likewise, the atmosphere in which arrows are aimed and released is vital. External conditions must be constantly monitored. Wind and other elements determine the success rate of an arrow reaching its desired target. This is true of our children. Since they are arrows, the environmental conditions must be conducive to their success. While aiming is critical, aiming them in the right surroundings is equally important. Never forget that the journey is as important as the destination. Destiny is a place that is reached by completing a journey. We live in a time when our children's environment is always dangerously affected. Media, people, relationships, and many other vehicles can taint the environment in which our children live and operate. Parents must monitor their children's relationships to the best of their ability. Social Media on any platform has to be constantly monitored. Cell phones and other communication instruments expose our children to many different types of people and circumstances that can adversely affect their aim and progress. Our children's activities and relationships must be scrutinized early. We must teach our children what is acceptable for them to engage in. We have always reminded our children to surround themselves with other young people who have related goals and dreams.

Parents must remember that a large part of parenting is on-the-job training. Unfortunately, many learn how from previous generations, in which dysfunction and emotional baggage have modeled flawed perspectives. Just as we study to become effective in our professional careers, we must study to show ourselves approved as parents. We must become professional parents. To become quality parents, we need time and tutoring.

Let's return to our metaphor once again. If children are arrows, parents must always desire to steward them with great care and protection. Arrows have to be examined often and maintained to remain proficient and effective. They must be sharpened. How, then, do we sharpen them? By modeling a life of character and integrity before them. Children become what they see! Children model the actions, language, and personalities of the adults that influence them. Parents should never underestimate the level of influence that they have over their children. In short, no one should have a more significant influence on our children's lives than we do. While our young people can have several role models, every parent should strive to become the best example of destiny and the most visible witness in our kids' lives. It is said that daughters marry their fathers, and sons marry their mothers. As parents, we must never forget that we are the inspiration that pushes our children to make decisions in life.

Destiny is the root word for destination. Every parent must ask where they believe God has called their child to end up and what the destination is. I'm not talking about their eternal redemption but their physical assignment and destined call. As a parent, I must see my child as an apprentice whom God has called me to prepare for the real-world assignment placed upon their life before they were formed in their mother's womb. Proverbs 22:6 (KJV) teaches this principle with purpose and divine insight. "Train up a child in the way he should go." I believe that no greater scripture can be found that becomes the formula for productive parenting. Parenting is a management position, first and foremost. We are their primary trainers. While teachers, ministers, coaches, and pastors impact our children, the chief responsibility of training resides with parents. No one should have a stronger influence on the life of your child. The term train implies teaching them what you know. Parents are to pour their knowledge and experience into their lives. Numerous times, I hear parents say, "I got mine. They have to get theirs." What a terrible parenting picture. I do not want my children to learn the lessons the way I did. I want to teach and train them so they can avoid the mistakes I made. Parents are managers first and are called to model life lessons for their children. Again, train them in the "way that they should go." Let children observe how we handle disappointments, make decisions, and process through challenges. I must remind parents that we lose our credibility when we live hypocritically in front of our offspring. They can spot a phony a mile away. Our example is our sermon: preach with your life, not your words.

I see so many parents trying to raise grown children. I hate to share, but it's too late. Parents need to take advantage of the momentum of parenting children, not adults. The Bible says to train up a "child." A young sapling can be bent, but a tree cannot. The best image of the potential of a child is a sponge. It absorbs at a rapid rate. Unfortunately, a sponge will absorb whatever it comes into contact with. Children are like sponges; they absorb everything we allow. Kids are pliable, changeable, and moldable. If you ask a child what they want to be when they grow up, it will change daily based on what they have been exposed to. We limit their minds and potential because we do not expose them to all that is available. Visiting your old elementary or high school is the perfect example of exposure. When you were a student, the halls looked large and long, but when you grow up and return, the halls look small and short. The halls are, in fact, the same, but you have been exposed to much larger environments.

Parenting is about management, modeling, and momentum. The committed parent is driven by a motivation that the principles of the Bible promise. The Bible declares that when we have been effective parents, our children will not depart from the precepts and principles that they have been taught. Proverbs 22 teaches us that they will not depart from it. Let me pause and give every parent who feels overwhelmed and ineffective an encouraging reminder that God's words have an eternal promise for parents. Every parent's motivation should be looking with anticipation for the day in which the fruit of their labor is evident in the product of a strong, productive adult child. Do not grow weary in well doing. Every lesson is a seed that has been sown into our children's future. Every moment of discipline is an investment in the harvest of a Christ-centered adult. Every word of correction is a moment of cultivation that will eventually produce fruit. Never give up on a child; they represent our greatest seed for a future of hope.

"The most important work you will ever do will be within the walls of your own home."

- Harold B. Lee

A Kingdom Parenting Approach
to Healing Generations and Transforming Legacies

Children And God

A child is a blessing from God, ensuring the existence of another generation. While we can participate in creating life, God ultimately decides to allow life to exist. We show our gratefulness to God by choosing to dedicate our child to him. I believe every child should be dedicated to God for several reasons. Dedicating a child is our outward expression of gratitude to God for allowing us to be a part of life's creative process. Secondly, a child should be dedicated as an expression of dependence. As parents, when we choose dedication, we essentially say we need help from the village to raise and steward this young life. Dedication is an invitation to grandparents, Godparents, and any other family and friends that we desire to stand with us and hold our arms up as we attempt to rear a productive adult. I am reminded of the scene in the historical novel and docuseries Roots in which the father holds up the child and declares, "Behold the only one greater than you," as a bold expression of honor for God and declaring inspiration for the child. And finally, dedication is the opportunity for intercession, a time in which we ask for the assistance of God. It can also serve as a time of instruction for the village extended, which may include reminding Godparents of their roles and responsibilities. The occasion is a time of seed-planting of faith. One of the things we do in our church is to write the child a letter to be safeguarded by the parents until the child is old enough to begin to ask questions about God and faith. The letter can be given then, reminding them that the village came together at a certain date, prayed over them, and planted seeds of faith. People often ask me where the ceremony takes place. While doing so in the local church is wonderful, scripture does not require it. While I believe that the local church has a distinct role in providing a ministry that assists parents in discipling their children, it is solely the parent's decision where the moment should take place and how formal it should be. Let's not become consumed with form over fashion. The point is to have a moment in which we begin a process of spiritual formation for our children. Remember, our offspring belong ultimately to God. As parents, we are given the assignment of stewardship, not ownership. I have been asked many times if I dedicate children born out of wedlock. My answer is absolutely! Often, you hear children born without their parents being married referred to as illegitimate. What a terrible term. There are no illegitimate children. Every child is legitimate. Every child holds the God-given assignment to be an answer to a problem on the earth. You are reading a book by a pastor whose parents were not married when he was conceived. Please know I am not condoning behavior that does not recognize and reverence the covenant of marriage; I am simply establishing the reality that life is a God-given privilege and that everything God creates is good.

Our children learn faith from what they see and hear from the adults in their village. Recently, on a family vacation, I observed the influence of parents and family on the next generation. My granddaughter Kennedy is just learning to talk. She can say Pop-Pop, Daddy, Momma, the names of her brothers, and several other simple words. But the word that she has learned that was surprising to us was "Hallelujah." Although she does not understand the word's meaning through association, she has determined it to be an expression released in church. She has heard it, seen it, and now repeats it.

Please understand that all of what I write about children and God is influenced by the reality that I am the son of a pastor. We also understand that faith's role in a child's life is paramount to a successful life development plan. Some think one can succeed without setting foot inside a church or declaring a covenant relationship with Christ. While I agree, I also fully believe that instilling in our children a desire to develop a spiritual life also provides another vehicle for developing needed life lessons about love, charity, relationships, and many other aspects of productive living.

As a child, my Sunday was consumed with church for the first 12 years. We would leave our home around 8:00 a.m. so that my father could visit the hospitalized sick members of our church congregation. We would then head to church for Sunday school at 10:00 am and church service at 11:00. Church would end around 1:30 p.m. Then we would visit the members of our church family and usually have dinner at a designated home. It would typically be around 5:00 pm when we returned home if we did not have an evening worship service. It was a total day of God, or should I say religion. There were also many other spiritual formation moments, such as Vacation Bible School, Baptist Training Union, and Christian Boys Club, our church's version of the Boy Scouts.

Today, there is very little spiritual formation provided for children. As parents, please remember again that our children are like sponges. My granddaughter is not yet a year old, but because of church, she can say amen, hallelujah, and praise the Lord. While she does not understand what that means, she hears others around her saying that a spiritual foundation has already begun to be instilled. The primary job of parents is to develop the next generation and their value systems. Church can be a great support system in achieving these goals, but it should not be the primary resource.

Whatever we give time and effort to becomes that which is given value. Where we spend our time and resources becomes the areas of life that our children value. Whether we have a plan or not, we teach our children our value system by what they see us invest in. If your days are spent consumed with working, then working becomes the most valuable. If you spend your days drinking, then drinking becomes a priority. The primary way in which we teach children is through our actions. If you drop your child off for children's church and, then go play golf, you teach them that golf is more valuable than God. The old proverb that actions speak louder than words is profoundly true. Suppose you attend worship weekly but display behavior that does not align with Kingdom principles. In that case, you are wasting your time attending church. Once again, attending church does not guarantee a strong biblical foundation; it simply reinforces what we display. The Bible-carrying cursing parent will ultimately teach their children to be hypocrites. Growing up in church helped me to recognize that religion breeds hypocrisy. We learn how to act in certain places at certain times rather than how to develop a core belief system that dictates our actions daily.

I must be transparent: I fell short regarding family Bible Studies, but I did attempt to display behavior consistent with what I believe the Bible teaches. One of the ultimate ways to introduce your children to the Kingdom of God is to provide them with a children's Bible early. Even if the Bible is predominately pictures, it begins to whet their appetite for the things of God. Once children learn to read, introducing them to the Bible is a great way to inspire reading and their relationship with God. Never forget that some of the most exciting stories to read are, in fact, in the Bible. Joseph and the coat of many colors. David and Goliath. The little boy with fish and loaves. Another great way to introduce our children to the Word is by reading it to them. The version in which we use must be child sensitive. I am not implying that the Bible should be pushed down our children's throats or be the only literature source used. Still, it should be a part of a healthy blend of reading resources. What I am attempting to convey, however, is that whatever we are reading to our children should be driven by agenda. Read to them with a Godly purpose. Not simply for the single-mindedness of inspiring a love for books and reading but for teaching and developing core beliefs for life. For instance, the story of David and Goliath teaches about decision-making, courage, self-confidence, etc. As parents, the Bible and other supplemental literature can teach about difficult subjects in our society, like racism, prejudice, and hatred. The Bible is more than a book I carry to church once a week; it is an excellent source of reinforcement for behavior, critical thinking, and shaping family values.

From the time a child is born, one of the chief responsibilities of a parent is shaping a belief system in the mind of the child. Children are like a blank whiteboard waiting for impressions to be drawn. These impressions are drawn by society, family, relationships, peers, and parents. As such, it should be our desire that no one has had more imprint on their belief system than we have. We must talk to our children and remind them often about what we believe. Let's take it a step further. Have you ever stopped to develop a family belief system plan? What do we believe about people? What do we believe about working? What do we believe about responsibilities? The list can be exhaustive, but you understand. Here is the major question. What does our family stand for? We worked hard to inspire our children to know what our family stood for and our family assignment on the earth. The primary vehicle for teaching belief systems is actions. Our children are givers because they saw that we were givers. Our children value education because, in their younger years, they saw us returning to school, making a sacrifice of working, raising a family, and traveling to school in other parts of the nation. A plan must be developed with strategic actions to inspire, teach, and develop a belief system for the next generation. As children become school-aged, the influence of people outside the home ramps up. Some studies suggest we receive over 1,000 impressions daily from our daily interactions. Repetitive reinforcement is the primary way to develop a belief system in our children. It must be consistently shared and modeled. We learn through repetition.

Every parent should take the time to explore a family genogram. This is a biological fingerprint of our bloodline. It provides a real portrait of the good, bad, and the ugly of your family history. Perhaps one of the realities of a genogram is to discover generational curses. As our children get older and develop, being honest about the areas in which our family struggles will assist the next generation in being proactive in addressing, attacking, and ending generational strongholds. In too many homes there is a failure to talk about generational curses. Ignorance sometimes causes us to fall victim to the unknown. I cannot watch out for what I have not identified. Be honest and open with the next generation so that they can be armed with the necessary tools to overcome the generational plans of Satan. We are called to break the cycles of alcoholism, divorce, sicknesses, and curses designed to prohibit future generations' prosperity.

Unfortunately, much of our influence over our children spiritually has created an intense spirit of religion. I grew up knowing how to do church, but only in my latter years did I discover the real meaning of developing a relationship with God. We are accountable as parents to display and teach our children how to develop a meaningful relationship with God. One of the greatest hindrances to teaching our children is found in the reality that parents don't have a genuine relationship of their own with God. Never forget that children are intelligent and can smell a fake. Our model is more important than what we say. When children see parents wrestling and developing their kingdom relationship with the eternal God, it gives them a visual foundation they can duplicate and develop into expressing their faith.

Children And Decision-Making

From the moment a child is born, lessons about decision-making are being taught, from the perils of sticking something in an electrical outlet to not touching hot stoves and pipes. As an adult, I recognize that our station in life can all be traced back to the total of our decisions. These choices are the foundation to destiny and become the guardrails to our future success. What appears to be simple and small decisions for a child become the training process for major life decisions later. All choices have impact and repercussions; none stand independent, but they have comprehensive and compounded implications. Our choices shape our value system, which then develops our process of thinking. It is important to remind our children that many decisions impact their future. We should be committed to helping them become independent thinkers and learn early how to handle peer pressure when making decisions.

When our daughter Kimberly was finishing her undergraduate degree, she wanted to attend a specific university to obtain her MBA. While it was a great institution, they did not offer her a total scholarship. However, another University offered her a full scholarship, room and board, health insurance, and a financial stipend to be a teacher assistant. It was decision time. Our daughter was adamant that she had to attend the first school. She informed us that we could afford to pay the difference in the funds needed after the partial scholarship. This was not about our ability to pay her tuition balance; it was an opportunity to display good stewardship in our decision-making. She was unhappy about our decision to send her to the school offering the full ride. After acquiring her degree, she enjoyed her time at the University, created and built life-long relationships, secured her MBA, and had supplemental finances for her future. This one decision set her up for bigger success in life. A small moment of disappointment was eventually overcome with the satisfaction of a sensible decision. Parents cannot become victims of familial peer pressure from their children. Stay the course, make sensible decisions, and empower the next generation to operate with fortitude and sound decision-making methods.

As a pastor, I often see the burden of student loans, over extended financial decisions that have crippled the future of God-fearing believers because no one ever assisted them with the appropriate wisdom concerning making decisions. I often tell people that I went to sleep one night at 25 and woke up the next morning at 60. The old hymn is correct, "Time is filled with swift transition." Time moves rapidly, and the apparent meaningless decisions of today will have more influence over the life we will live in the future.

One of the greatest mistakes parents make is protecting their children from the results of bad decision-making. To shield our kids from pain, we prevent them from learning real-life lessons about taking personal responsibility for decisions. We live in a bail-out society, where people desire to live however they want but expect to be rescued when their results are unfavorable. This creates a co-dependent, soft generation that blames someone else for their circumstances and will always need to be rescued from the effects of their poor decisions. In high school, I played on the basketball team my sophomore year. I worked hard and finally made my way into some substantial playing time. The day I was informed that I would get to play was also the day that report cards came out. The rule in our house was that you could not participate in sports if you received a grade below C on your report card. As fate would have it, I received a D in History during that marking period. I had made the decision not to study as diligently as required. It was my decision. When my mother received my grading report, she confidently communicated that I would not be allowed to play in the game that night. I remember informing her that I was eligible by the school system's standards. She reaffirmed that the school's standard was not hers. Because this was such a tough decision for my mom, she went to bed early that evening to prevent having to see my disappointment. I did not play that night and never again worked my way into the playing rotation. But I learned a valuable lesson. During the next marking period, my grade in history was a B. Stop bailing our children out. While we think we are preventing them from pain, we are robbing them of vital lessons required to succeed. The court system, banks, and society will hold them accountable for decisions. The earlier we teach young people to learn this difficult lesson, the more productive they will be. Spend time talking with your children about their decisions. Take the opportunity to discuss the decisions of others and the obvious implications of those decisions as moments of training and insight. Raise up models where decisions were made that had a positive impact. It is important to have real-life examples as vehicles of instruction before those situations are presented. We can learn from the mistakes of others and become motivated not to make the same mistakes that have been made in the past. While it can be difficult to share our shortcomings, it can be very meaningful to communicate how our decisions as parents have had both positive and negative impacts on us. Transparency can become an excellent catalyst for growth. We should not want the next generation to repeat the lessons we learned. Our mistakes can and should be used to train the next generation to become more effective decision-makers.

"Brilliant ideas pay off and bring you prosperity,

but making hasty, impatient decisions

will only lead to financial loss."

- Proverbs 21:5 (TPT)

Children: Finances And Work

As a child, I remember Saturday mornings when my grandfather and uncle would pick me up early. They were carpenters by trade and would take me to job sites where I would serve as a laborer and assistant to them as they accomplished the task of the day. My grandfather would make several statements that are still fresh in my mind. One statement would be that if a man learns a trade, no one can ever take that away from him. Another was if a man does not work, he does not eat. It is the premise of these two statements that have shaped what I believe about children and work. One of the sad realities is that if I were to go into the average child's bedroom, I would find a closet full of sneakers, perhaps worth thousands of dollars, video games worth hundreds of dollars, cell phones, computers, and televisions they did not work for. We have created an environment of entitlement. As I examine our society and observe the behavior of many of our young people, it is clear that, as parents, we have failed to teach them strong work ethics. I'm sure many of us remember Saturday mornings when we could not go out and play until we had taken care of our daily and weekly chore assignments.

I fondly remember my brother and me turning on the radio and listening to music. At the same time, we scrubbed the kitchen floor, swept the front and back porches, dusted all of the what-nots that rested on my grandmother's living room tables, and checked off the responsibilities of the day. In Second Kings chapter 4, there is a story of a widow. The foundation of the story is the fact that the creditors are coming to get her children. They are coming to take her boys as slaves. I suggest that just as that woman in the Bible was in debt over her head and her children were bonded to slavery, we today find that because we have not managed our work ethics, we have affected the next generation's legacy. There is a lesson that we can learn from this woman. A part of her healing and deliverance, or should I say the healing and deliverance for her family, was built around the reality that her child had an assignment. You'll notice that she is told to send her child to all of the neighbors to borrow vessels. Children must be taught early on that they have responsibility and assignment in the family's development and legacy. Unfortunately, so many parents fail to consistently remember they are called to train the next generation, and one of their responsibilities is to teach healthy work ethics. Let's stop just for a moment and explore the concept of allowance. Almost all parents provide an allowance for their children. It is an amount of money given to their children, perhaps weekly or monthly, as their financial blessing. The term allowance communicates a reality that does not align with how the world operates. Could we be teaching them to operate with unrealistic expectations by providing it? Let's think about it: every Friday or every other Friday, our children come to us and receive a set amount of money that we call an allowance. Suppose there is no structured activity connected to the receiving of those funds. In that case, we are teaching our children that they will receive compensation for having accomplished nothing. The problem with this kind of teaching is that no Corporation will pay them weekly, biweekly, or monthly for accomplishing nothing when they become adults and work in the real world. One of the reasons why so many young people have weakened or reduced work ethics is that we have created an environment that does not connect compensation to responsibility. A single change can begin to teach lifelong work ethics and develop positive work habits that will enable our kids to be so much more productive in society. As a parent, I would suggest developing a job description with definitive responsibilities and assignments. Upon sitting down with them, establish the compensation that will be received based on completing the assignments and responsibilities developed. Since we are attempting to teach young people real-world lessons, they will be compensated fully as they complete the tasks. For example, suppose one of the duties is making up the bed, and they make the bed up three days out of the week. In that case, their compensation should be adjusted based on the amount of the assignment that was completed. Is that not how it works in the real world? If you work three days a week, you are paid for three days. We teach them several lessons by using this methodology when children are young. We teach them that nothing in life is free. We also teach them that they control their destiny.

When our children were young, they were required to work at the church as their service to the community.

On a particular day, my daughter was assigned to the ministry bookstore, preparing CDs for the next Sunday's sales. She was duplicating and labeling the CD's. Upon stopping by the church to check on her, I found her sleeping in my office. I woke her up and reminded her about her responsibility in the bookstore. Her response to me was, "I'm not getting paid." I adamantly reminded her that the bed she slept in at night, the food she ate, and the clothes she wore were all provided for because of the ministry and church we served. Today, she is full-time in the ministry. She oversees the business arm of the fellowship, including the delivery of books and ministry materials. She learned early to pick up sticks like the woman and her children in 1st Kings 17.

As parents, we must never forget that our chief responsibility is raising up another generation. Your son will become someone's husband, and your daughter will become someone's wife. To that end, we must take seriously our responsibility as the chief instructors in their lives to equip and prepare them for life to the best of our ability. For children, chores are one of the ways to shape strong and genuine work ethics. Chores should be consistent, written, and communicated so they will fully understand what is expected. It becomes vitally important that our young are taught how to establish goals and objectives for life. One of the ways that we can teach our children the value of goal setting is by connecting work, compensation, and the successful attainment of goals. If a child desires a new pair of sneakers, rather than simply paying for the sneakers, allow the sneakers to become a goal and connect the compensation required to purchase the sneakers to chores around the home. Doing this will teach the child goal setting, work ethic, and decision-making. It is always interesting to note that most people, even our children, think differently when spending their money. It is so much easier to spend the money of others. Not only will this begin to shape their work ethic, but it will also serve as a catalyst for building self-esteem. Setting a goal and then achieving that goal is one way that our confidence and our motivation to continue to strive to be all that we can be is developed.

A recent survey from the makers of the chore app BusyKid found that while more than 90 percent of parents say they did chores as a child, only 66 percent regularly have their children do chores. I clearly remember how Mrs. Battle, the older neighbor across the street from us, would call my mom and ask if I could walk to the neighborhood store and pick up some merchandise for her. My Mom would volunteer me without my approval and then inform me that I would not accept compensation from Mrs. Battle for making the trip. While I would be upset at my Mom then, I now understand that my mom was teaching me the concept of service and volunteering. Unfortunately, we live in a time where children rarely do anything for free. My generation was required to serve the community church and accomplish household chores. We must return to teaching our children to live with a sensitivity of service. Gandhi once said, "The best way to find yourself is to lose yourself in the service of others." Service often acts as a compass for our future and the purpose of life. As a teenager, I served in Third Baptist Church by driving the Sunday school van, operating the video camera, and singing in the choir. I believe the reason I am so passionate about serving the Kingdom today is that I had to serve the Kingdom as a young person. When parents begin to see areas of purpose reveal themselves, we must push our children to volunteer in areas that feed that purpose.

By teaching our children to volunteer, we train a spirit of empathy. In a world driven by selfishness, volunteering helps them to see the needs of others as a priority. Putting your neighbor first is a lost concept in our society today. Another advantage of volunteerism is training them to work with others effectively. Skills such as communication and collaboration are sharpened by fostering an environment of service. As parents, we must train the next generation to be civic-minded and help them understand the need to give back to the community in which they live. When much is given, much is required. The act of service and volunteering will also produce a great attitude of thanksgiving. When we volunteer, it causes us to take a reality check and recognize how blessed we are.

I am always impressed by the young people who serve in our church. I acknowledge that sometimes serving creates a platform for career experience. For example, serving in our creative arts department can provide a tremendous experience for those wanting to pursue a career in the arts, television, or theater.

Making my bed, taking out the trash, cleaning the bathroom, cutting the grass, and washing the dishes were all assigned to me as a child. I was, in fact, an indentured servant. My mother was serious about chores. Today, many children have no household assignments. I would suggest that we have created a soft next generation that will struggle to provide for their family. Chores are not just assignments to help the home run smoother; chores have a much deeper value than we typically acknowledge. Chores teach young people vital life skills. I still hear my mother saying, I'm teaching you to cook so you will never have to depend on anyone to eat. To this day, I have skills in the kitchen that surprise my children. Thank you, Mom. Another reason chores are important is because they teach our children responsibility and self-worth. It creates a spirit of self-confidence, boosts their self-esteem, and gives them a sense of accomplishment. Perhaps one of the most unspoken benefits of chores is teaching children to respect authority. My mother would tell me that when she got home from work, she wanted the dishes clean, the grass cut, my room cleaned, etc. Although I would wait until the last minute to accomplish those tasks, I would not allow her to walk in the door, leaving them undone. Although I was bigger than my mother, I had a healthy respect for her position as the boss of the house. She was, in fact, my mother and my employer. That respect I learned as a child has trained my behavior as a pastor. I have great respect for those who have authority over me. My apostolic authority and the elders never have to be concerned about my respect for them because it was ingrained in me as a child. My mother would get home from work between 5:30 and 6:00 p.m. I learned how to complete my homework and finish my chores by the time she set foot in the door. Time management was vicariously taught by accomplishing my chores. I did not have time to get in trouble. Remember the old proverb, "Idle hands are the devil's workshop." Remember that you cannot wait until the child is a teenager to assign chores. It must start when they are young. Age-appropriate chores can create a culture of accountability and discipline. Finally, one of the most important lessons that chores teach is self-reliance. Children with chores grow up being more independent in their thinking and typically become leaders and not just followers. In a world where everyone tends to blame someone else or expect someone to rescue them, chores can become a great character builder and create a personality of strength. A 75-year Harvard University study examined the childhood psychosocial variables and biological processes that predicted health and well-being later in life. Researchers concluded that kids who had chores fared better later in life. Like the women in 1st and 2nd Kings, we are responsible for teaching our children to pick up sticks and bring us the vessels to provide oil. Work never killed anyone.

"Teach your children the value of a dollar, but also that true wealth comes from wise financial choices and a generous heart."

-Anonymous

Children And Money

When our children were in their early teenage years, we lived on a private golf course and country club. My son had started to play high school golf and needed to be able to use the course to practice. Because the course was private, you had to be a member to play. We could not afford to play, so I secured a job for my son as the person who would take care of the carts several days a week. The day my son was to begin, his mother sat him down and shared that he was not working to obtain money to purchase sneakers and other needs. As his parents, we were responsible for providing for his needs. He was starting this job to learn how to develop a work ethic. His mother then taught him what I believe is one of the most important life lessons we can teach our children about money. She shared that he was never to ask his boss for his paycheck. Never let your boss know that you need the check. Several weeks later, I bumped into the club teaching pro and asked him how my son was doing on the job. He informed me that he was well-mannered and doing a great job. He then told me he had two months of paychecks in his mailbox at the course because he had never picked them up. No one had ever told my son that he had a company mailbox. I was proud of my son, for he had learned the lesson and began his occupational career with focus and fortitude.

Perhaps one of the saddest stations in life is to have worked all of your life and, when you are aged, have nothing to show for years of effort. I am not saying that life is summed up by possessions. Still, I am suggesting that we should have something to show for the time we have invested in working when we have been blessed with the favor of old age. However, it is not our fault because we have not been exposed to financial principles and taught economic structure. When children are small, they have no clear comprehension of money. If you offer a small child ten quarters or the choice of a 20-dollar bill, they will most likely choose the ten quarters because it appears to be more. While that is acceptable reasoning for a small child, having a warped sense of finance is not acceptable for young adults. Remember, we don't know what we don't know. We teach our children to catch a ball, make those first steps, and recognize their colors. Yet most families never take seriously the need to teach them about money.

When my son was young, we asked him which family in our circle of relationships he desired to live like as an adult. He instantly named one of the families in our church who had been blessed to have successful careers. The husband was a retired Army officer, and his wife was an educator in our school system. He drove a Corvette, and the wife drove a Lexus SUV. They both had college degrees, lived in a beautiful home, and vacationed where and when they desired. We immediately asked my son how much income he thought was required to live at the level where he saw them living. His answer was amazing to us. His answer revealed that he had no real concept of how economics worked and the accurate cost of living. A simple exercise was developed to attempt to help him understand. We pulled out the tried-and-true family game called Monopoly. After giving him the amount of money he had suggested as acceptable to live on, we developed a budget based on the couple's lifestyle. At the end of the month, he was broke! This simple exercise can teach children about financial decision-making and help them understand the need to go to college and how to shape their thinking about money and finance. We saw the beginning of a shift of thinking when it was time to purchase his sneakers and back-to-school clothing. It helped to lay the groundwork for his financial thinking as an adult.

As a part of community outreach, our church decided to pay off the student lunch debt in our city. We discovered that in our city, which portrays itself as a middle-class city economically, $30,000 was the balance owed by students for charging their lunch money. It never occurred to me that students who were living beneath the poverty line received free lunch as a student, which meant that any amount that we charged had to come from students who were not necessarily in need. I was shocked to find out how many students lived in beautiful homes and had parents who drove very nice cars but could not afford to pay for their lunch. Numerous parents overextend themselves trying to impress people or satisfy places of woundedness from their childhood that have gone unhealed.

Economic situations are a direct result of economic baggage from our childhood. We did pay off the student lunch loan debt in our city, but I could not help but wonder how long it would be before the amount was high once again because we were not addressing the real problem, which was a lack of good economic decision-making by parents.

Can I pause and ask you some questions? What do you drive? How large is your home? Do you spend a lot of money on depreciating assets like clothes and shoes? Do you have a well-thought-out retirement plan for your future? Do you have six months of income saved? Does your child have a college fund? What happens when you are confronted with a health challenge in the future? Do you have life insurance? While these questions might make us uncomfortable, they must be answered. Finding honest answers to these questions is the beginning of developing a strategy to teach our children how to handle money.

As parents, we have moments of major purchases, such as buying a car or home, that can also serve as great opportunities to teach our children about money and finance. As our children became teenagers, we thought it was important to allow them to be present at those times so they could learn critical economic lessons. For most of us, the first time we purchase a car is the first time we have ever been a part of a car purchasing process. No wonder people end up with high interest rates and long loan periods. We have not been trained or educated. Moments like these present a unique opportunity to teach about interest rates and other pertinent financial principles. I have found that if we don't take advantage of these moments, we shortchange our children and not provide them with adequate tools for future financial success.

Another way to teach children financial lessons is to adopt a method where parents act as a bank. For example, When they want the latest sneakers rather than you simply buying them, play the role of the bank, allowing your children to finance the purchase. Give them a 100-dollar loan and sign a loan agreement with the repayment plan explained. Define when payments must be made and spell out the interest rate. Just like in real life, if they decide to make a decision with their money that prevents them from paying their bill, the shoes must be repossessed. This simple exercise teaches real-life lessons and begins to train financial decision-making.

One of the moments that was always so frustrating for me was spending a large amount of money on toys for Christmas morning only to hear your children declare by the afternoon, "I'm bored." This declaration would be made while sitting among a pile of boxes that had been opened; the trash piled up on the floor from toy boxes that had been opened and toys that had been played with for five minutes. While our family room looked like a toy store, our children pouted and said they had nothing to do. This reality prompted us to start a new family tradition—the Christmas morning scavenger hunt. We decided not to put any gifts under the tree; instead, we hid all the gifts we had purchased. We then provided our children with clues to the hiding places of their gifts. We only gave them clues for one gift at a time to make this activity a day-long challenge. They could not proceed to the next gift until they found the previous one. It would take most of the day to provide a special family bonding time and teach the value of the gifts and our financial sacrifice. Developing creative strategies like this creates a platform for teaching appreciation and financial principles that can create lasting memories for our children.

An area of finance that we miss is the opportunity to teach and inspire our children about giving. As a believer, giving is a major component of my financial belief system. I am responsible for assisting my children in understanding the value of developing a spirit of benevolence. This does not simply include teaching them about giving to the church but also becoming sensitive to giving to others. When our children were small, we would teach them the principles of giving with intentionality at Christmas. They were responsible for selecting a family or individual to give to during the holiday. They chose an older lady in our congregation named E. M. Gray one Christmas. Sister Gray had come through some difficult seasons and had gone to prison in her young adult life. She was a regular attender of worship and would always wear a hat on Sundays. Our children decided to buy Sister Gray a new hat for Christmas. They designated a portion of their Christmas savings as the amount they would spend on the purchase. We traveled to the local store where the church ladies purchased their Sunday best hats and acquired a beautiful white hat. On Christmas Eve, we drove to her modest home and left the hat in a beautiful hat box on her porch. The pride that I saw in my children's eyes that Sunday when Sister Gray walked into church wearing her new white hat, is still clearly etched in my mind. But that's not the end of the story. When the Lord called Sister Gray home, she told her family she wanted to be buried in her white hat. As a parent, I felt a sense of parental pride when I viewed her body lying in her casket with the hat my children had purchased, crowning her head. To this day, we still speak about that Christmas every year as we spend family time together.

As stewards of our children's financial future, we should always attempt to keep them grounded with information that can be used as an instrument of instruction to equip them to be successful when they become adults. Allow them to be a part of developing the household budget or observing the monthly bank statements. Sitting down with our young people and working through the monthly bank statement is a marvelous way of teaching them the value of spending. At the same time, this simple exercise teaches our children realistically what it takes to operate a home. Reviewing the bank statement will also allow parents to explore where the household resources are spent each month. If you want to go further, you can take the monthly bank statement and create a simple bar chart to visualize where we spend our income. Whenever cereal is left in the bowl, or a glass of orange juice is left half full, we can teach the value of things we take for granted.

I have discovered that one of the hardest financial lessons to teach a child is the principle of saving. The earlier we can begin to teach them to save, the more probable it becomes that this will create a mentality of saving when they are adults. When our children were young, it was not uncommon for them to have a significant amount of money after celebrating special days like birthdays, Christmas, and graduations. They would begin dreaming about what to use the money to purchase. I will never forget their lack of enthusiasm when we informed them they were required to save some money.

We would decide how much they could spend and how much they were required to save. This would be helpful with the decision to spend in the future. I found out that our children were not as excited about spending their savings to purchase sneakers as they were about spending my money to make the same purchase. Secondary to the concept of savings was the principle of tithing. Very early, we began to teach our children the value of tithing. I am proud that today, our children are grown, and they still display the reality of these teachings as they practice saving and tithing. While these practices have a distinct value in our spiritual development, they also teach financial discipline and develop a systematic structure to increase the probability of financial success as adults.

"Wise men and women are always learning, always listening for fresh insights."

-Proverbs 18:15 (MSG)

A Kingdom Parenting Approach
to Healing Generations and Transforming Legacies

Children And Education

The first and most impactful teacher in your child's life should be you as the parent. Parents are the original source of instruction in the life of their child. No one should have greater influence than you. I challenge every parent reading this today to stop and think about their parental weight. How we live our lives can either increase or decrease this influence. As our children become school-aged, it is important to remember that every child is distinctively different. Years ago, almost every parent was a member of the PTA. The other day, I talked with an educator, and she informed me that they do membership drives intending to get 50 percent of parents involved in the PTA. As parents, our presence in their lives is more important than money, toys, or material possessions. Time is our most valuable commodity. The parent-teacher relationship is vital to the success of our children. Far too often, parents don't have the time to invest in their children's educational progress because they are consumed by their careers. The decision to have children is a decision to reprioritize life. Once children enter a family, we are accountable for stewarding that life with intentionality, structure, and time. A parent should know their children's teachers and take full advantage of parent-teacher days, PTA meetings, and any other opportunities to be present in their school. My wife and I were involved in their educational journey when our children were young. We both have served as room parents and were active leaders in developing a strategy for our children to succeed. It is much more productive for your child's educators to know you because of your activity and participation than your involvement only in disciplinary situations.

Allow me to stop and remind every parent about the reality of being a teacher. They are overworked, underpaid, and more than likely have student debt from their matriculation, and believe it or not, your child is not the only student they are responsible for. Add on the reality that they have their own family and children. When I was little, the teacher was always right until proven wrong. Today, in most situations, the teacher is wrong until proven right. What are some simple things I, as a parent, can do to make my children successful in their educational journey? I am glad you asked. Develop an educational calendar for the year. Place all the essential dates on this calendar, such as grading periods, parent-teacher meetings, and other specified times. Other pertinent periods that are important to record and track are dates of standardized tests. This allows the family to shape its activities around these moments. My mother knew when report cards came out and would request them on arrival home from her workday. This calendar can be placed on the refrigerator so that the times are visible and tracked. This allows parents to establish and manage their career calendars in relationship to their children's schedules. Parents should also establish educational boundaries for their children. What are the household rules about homework? As a child, the first thing I did upon arriving home after school was to change from my "school clothes." Most of us had "play clothes." They were usually the old clothes that no longer fit. Then secondly, it was clear that we were not allowed to go outside until all homework had been completed. What are the household rules on grades? Grades are not given for the benefit of the teacher but for the benefit of the student and parents. The parents are responsible for having a daily routine in which homework is checked, and the daily activity is the center of the dialogue.

Nothing has impacted our children's education more than the erosion of family time and family dinners. Dinner was the time to discuss the day and what happened at school. Because of a grave change in lifestyle, dinner hours are very segregated. Everyone eats dinner in a different place at a different time, which becomes a barrier to family communication and sharing. Parents work late; children have activities and clubs. Understanding how life has changed, it becomes even more important for parents to build time in the family schedule for sharing and engaging with one another. We plan for everything else in our life. We have to become very proactive in planning how the family will engage to ensure our children have every ability to succeed in their academic journey.

The educational journey is not all about grades and academic matriculation. The educational atmosphere also provides an opportunity to teach our children about relationships. Learning to respect people such as the bus driver, the custodian, and the cafeteria worker is an imperative lesson to teach our young. Learning to respect everyone in authority is vital, and parents bear the responsibility of teaching their children these important life lessons.

As I observe families today, from the role of a parent and a pastor, I cringe when I see parents who are not desirous or able to invest their time in the special days of their children. Special days are just that, special days. I remember hearing the saints sing, "Time is filled with swift transition," as a child. What that means is time is not redeemable. You don't get a do-over for missed moments in their lives. Just as you will never see them take their first step again, you will never see them lead the Pledge of Allegiance again or shoot the winning free throw in a ball game again. While I am aware that circumstances sometimes prevent us from being present, that should be the exception and not the norm. At the end of the day, your child desires time with you, to see you present, to know that you value their activities.

One of the greatest blessings of serving as a pastor for over three decades is seeing families grow. Baptizing and dedicating babies who have become functional adults is the reward of pastoral service. While there have been many family success stories in our church, one family has provided a blueprint for shaping the thinking and development of the next generation through a family creed. Every morning before the children in this family would leave for school, the parents would lead them in reciting their family creed at the front door. They would conclude the moment with family prayer. I watched from a distance as this creed became the statement that governed their daily activities. As parents, sit down with your children and corporately write your family creed. In this statement, you could include values, core beliefs, and expectations for behavior. Develop a strategy for leaving the home every morning to start the day as a family. You can create this devotional moment for your family in different ways. Each member of the family can take a turn leading the prayer. Perhaps you can add a moment where the family designated a word for the day, such as "serve, share, integrity," allowing the word to become the guiding instrument for the day. The benefits of this intentional beginning to each day are endless. It creates focus, develops family interaction, shapes our thinking, and constantly reminds us to reflect on personal responsibility. It builds and creates a relationship bond that enables the family to handle the events and stresses of daily duties and responsibilities in all areas of life.

One of the concerns that has become a grave source of concern as we observe children today is the lack of participation in extra-curricular activities. I recently spoke with an educator who informed me they are having difficulty fielding athletic teams because of a lack of student engagement. One of the main reasons there is such a low participation rate in extra-curricular activities is that young people often work jobs to provide for expensive clothing, cars, and cell phones. When I was in high school, the highlight of the week was attending the Friday night football games and being a part of the community of students that became an extended system of support. Participating in after-school activities should be a priority for parents for several reasons. First, it supplies a platform for young people to explore their gifts and abilities. Unfortunately, most parents are only concerned with athletics, but there are many other activities that young people can participate in. Because every child is distinctively different, these activities become beneficial in guiding and equipping young people to embrace their God-given abilities. Secondly, extra activities provide an opportunity for young people to become more effective at developing interpersonal relationship skills. Cultivating relationships teaches empathy, compromise, and teamwork. Finally, extra-curricular activities can also teach valuable lessons about life, such as hard work handling disappointment and difficulty, while training young people to respect authority and leadership. Our sociological desire for material possessions has created a culture that defines itself by materialism. Parents are responsible for guiding their children to participate in extra activities and determining which activities best complement the gifts and abilities recognized in the child.

My son played high school golf, and my daughter played high school basketball. They learned many lessons from themselves and their parents; the greatest unexpected lessons were developing perseverance and commitment. When my daughter was not getting the playing time that she thought she deserved and desired to switch to other clubs and activities, I reminded her that we don't quit. Teaching the next generation how to remain committed amid adversity is important. When my son played golf in a national tournament and did not play as well as he could, he did not want to finish the tournament. Once again, I reminded him we do not quit in the Brown family. He also learned that other young people who performed better were not necessarily better than him. They simply had a more committed work ethic and practiced at a level that he did not. These are all valuable lessons that they learned early and have continued to be guided by to this day.

I am often asked which is best for our children: Christian School, Private School, or Public School. My answer might surprise you. I think each of them has a place and a purpose, and the decision of where to place your child should be driven by a clear understanding that each child is different. Our daughter attended a Christian private school in the early years of her educational journey, and our son went to public school. Both have done very well and have become well-rounded adults. Public schools usually provide a more balanced picture of society than many private schools. Unfortunately, many parents enroll their children in Christian schools to discipline them in the faith. Let me remind parents that educators, even in a Christian school environment, should never become the chief discipliner of our children. Parents are the original pastors and spiritual leaders of their children. Regardless of the choice, parents' continual involvement in their children's academic journey is required and should not be compromised. The final decision about the intellectual atmosphere in which a child will be entrusted should ultimately be made based on academic excellence, the child's ability, and personality. Parents must see the educational setting as a place of cultivation socially, academically, and emotionally. I advise parents always to explore all available options and make the best decision possible. The choice of a school should not be a status statement but a decision that best serves the future and destiny of the child. Families have mortgaged their future by paying high tuition when the local public school system provides high-quality education. Education is a vital component of the training of our children and should be given much consideration as we always attempt to do what is best for the child.

A Kingdom Parenting Approach
to Healing Generations and Transforming Legacies

Lastly, parents should supply input on how children pursue higher levels of education. Allow me to give you something to think about. Data informs us that people with a degree are half as likely to be unemployed as their peers with only a high school diploma. Individuals with a degree make an estimated 1.2 million dollars more than their peers with no degree over an average lifetime. As a parent, I am proud that our children have acquired college degrees. I am confident that their education has prepared them to be productive. However, before you crucify me, please understand that college is not for everyone and does not guarantee success in life. I am simply suggesting that parents take an active role in the educational decision-making of their children. As we make educational decisions remember that each child is different. One of the academic failures of many parents is allowing their children to enter into financial bondage with student loans. When my son graduated from high school, he made it clear that he was not ready for college and did not desire to waste our money. Today he has a graduate degree and no student debt. Parents need to remember that although technically your child is an adult when making decisions about college, they still need guidance. Talk to your adult children about all the dynamics of their decision-making. If you feel unqualified to give sound guidance solicit the assistance of someone credible so that they can make the best decision for their future.

Children: Family And Discipline

One day, while speaking with a juvenile judge in our city, she said something about discipline that has stuck with me until today. She mentioned how children stand before her on the bench with the same expectations about punishment that they have learned from their parent's behavior. Let me explain. When a parent gives the parameters of their prescribed discipline and does not follow through with the plan, they create a mentality of expectation. Children then stand before the judge, hear a declaration of the parameters of discipline, and wrongly expect the judge to commute their sentence like their parents did, only to find out that the judicial system does not work that way. Parents create unrealistic expectations when they do not hold the line and follow through on the administered restriction plans for their young. Many times, parents distribute discipline without stopping to consider how the discipline will affect the lifestyle of the family. For example, Taking away driving privileges from a child responsible for driving their sibling to appointments can become an additional burden to parents and often becomes the source of redirecting the parameters of the discipline itself.

Words are essential in every organization, especially in the family. We use many different terms to articulate parental discipline. Punishment and restriction are two of the most used terms. Because words convey thoughts and ideas, we must carefully use language to convey the concept of discipline we desire. I use restriction and discipline rather than punishment. The key to any established discipline plan must be correcting behavior and teaching respect for authority. As parents, we are the primary authority figures in the home, and helping our children learn the proper boundaries concerning authority will directly transfer into the external relationships in their lives, like educators and police officers.

One of the biggest mistakes I have witnessed parents make when it comes to discipline is making decisions in a vacuum without the input of both parents. Often, parents get caught up in the moment and issue discipline without properly thinking through the plan and the ability to enforce the discipline that has been administered. Taking time to unwind, calm down, and explore all of the situational information provided can assist in properly evaluating the form and function of the needed discipline. It is much more effective if parents train not to be reactive based on emotions. Emotions can improperly taint our reasoning and listening capabilities. Always ask yourself if the discipline fits the transgression of behavior that has taken place. In layperson's terms, does the penalty fit the crime?

Another area where parents have to manage the discipline process is consistency. I have kids who grow up with family relational baggage because discipline was not administered consistently. This is common in blended families where biological and bonus children are not treated equally. At times, this is because of past relational baggage from previous relationships in the life of parents that have caused them to operate with shaded perspectives and guilt. Unresolved emotional baggage in a parent's life has often been the catalyst for overbearing discipline or lack thereof. When evaluating parental discipline, one of the most important attributes is consistency. Children need and desire consistency and become confused by inconsistency. Allowing some moments without proper discipline creates an atmosphere that prevents proper accountability and does not teach life lessons that ensure success as adults.

Many parents have created an atmosphere of discipline that can best be described as good cop bad cop. There must be a balance between parents in how correction is administered. My father was the usual source of discipline in my home. Several of us grew up in a home where the statement from our mother was, "Wait until your father gets home." Allowing this type of disciplined process to exist will create a culture of preference between parents and children and leave lasting trauma that will often not fully be exposed until adulthood. When parents don't balance the discipline, it can cultivate a feeling of resentment toward the parent, who becomes the primary source of discipline.

Discipline must also be progressive. That means that doing the same form and type of discipline without behavioral improvement is ineffective. After all, the reason for discipline is to change behavior. An adjustment must be made if the administered discipline is not achieving the needed behavior change. The answer does not always lie in increasing the amount of discipline, but many times, a change in discipline. I believe the Bible teaches that corporal discipline is an acceptable method of addressing negative and unacceptable behavior. However, every child does not respond to this form of discipline, and every moment of inappropriate behavior does not warrant a physical discipline response.

When there is a need to determine the level of appropriate discipline, it can be much more effective for parents to come together and communicate their disappointment with their child. The next step should be conversing with each other without the child present. Once the parents agree on the type and level of discipline, they should always try to share the decision. This is very important once children have become older. It creates a culture of mutual respect and authority in the home, where both parents are recognized as authority figures. The language to share the decisions should always be we decided, instead of your mom or your dad decided.

I have so many different terms for the style and types of discipline. I think the most appropriate term is restriction. Punishment brings with it a connotation of a type of discipline that is institutional. As parents, we are attempting to restrict our children's negative behavior and create new patterns of behavior. Never forget that the true purpose of discipline is training and teaching that all decisions in life have repercussions.

There are times when our communication gap is evident when we share our expectations with our children. I remember an incident that took place when my son was young. Our children always had chores and household responsibilities. This particular day, I noticed that my son had not taken out the trash. I clearly communicated that I wanted him to take the trash out of the kitchen trash can as I left the house to run an errand. When I returned to the house approximately one hour later, the trash can was still full. I immediately began to rebuke him for his disobedience, only to have him reply that I had told him to take the trash out. Still, I did not put time parameters on the request. I did not say to take the trash out "now." He informed me that he intended to take the trash out when he was dressed and leaving to go outside. While I am sure he understood that I desired him to take the garbage out when the request was made, I had to acknowledge that he had a point. I did not communicate clearly. Always attempt to be as clear as possible when giving directions. If you were on the receiving end of the communication, would you understand the task and responsibility? Perhaps the best way to determine clarity is to ask, "Am I clear? Do you understand?"

"While a family may break apart, a child's heart is resilient. In the tapestry of life, even the threads of divorce can weave strength, growth, and a new beginning for every child."

-Anonymous

Children And Divorce

One of the most important components of helping your child understand divorce is to begin with clear communication. The children should be talked to as soon as the decision to divorce has been made. Both parents should sit down in an atmosphere that is neutral and calming. My suggestion is not to have this meeting in the home but in a pre-determined space that does not increase the stress of the conversation. It can also be valuable to do the meeting with the involvement of a counselor or other professional, such as a minister or pastor. At this meeting, several objectives should be accomplished. First, the meeting should clarify that the child is not the reason for the divorce. Secondly, the communication should be clear about how the future will look. One of the most important things to remember in this season is the need for love and assurance. Allow the child to share their perspective without becoming offended and overly emotional. Is one parent moving away? Will both parents remain in the area? How will living arrangements happen? Without going into the details of the parental relationship, communication should be as straightforward as possible about how the future looks. Never forget, the children have questions and are affected as much as the parents.

Parents must establish guidelines for engaging their children when moving through divorce. I married into a blended family as well as the product of divorce as a twelve-year-old child. From that time, I never visited my father at his home and had limited interaction with him until the day he died. One of my greatest regrets is that I do not have a picture of me and my dad. Because my dad was a pastor, their divorce was public and filled with tremendous sadness.

One of the most significant responsibilities of parents during and after divorce is protecting the children emotionally. Parents must be very protective about who they allow to supervise their children. The extended family and village can often be a source of dysfunction for children. People talk. Parents have to guard their kid's hearts by limiting those they are influenced by. Extended family conversations can be dangerous and leave life-long emotional wounds. As parents, we must clearly define the parameters in place for our extended families to safeguard their emotional strength. While closely studying the relationships of family and friends, it might become a requirement that some relationships are redefined for their mental health. There are times when I share with a couple moving through divorce, and they inform me that they are attending counseling. I believe counseling is an integral part of the healing process. Counseling can bring clarity to emotional concerns that have been hidden and be a source of personal revelation that leads to awareness of areas that require growth for future relationship success. However, I am amazed that some parents will enroll themselves in counseling but are reluctant to enroll their children. I suggest that counseling be provided individually for all involved and that counseling also take place for the family as a whole. Individual and family counseling allows a platform for conversation, growth, and healing that can provide needed tools for all involved to come through the divorce with less post-divorce baggage. Children should be encouraged to express their true feelings without fear of retribution from each parent. Perhaps the most significant relationship detriment I have noticed during divorce is when one of the parents expresses the mistakes the other parent has made. For instance, sharing with the child that a parent has been morally unfaithful is an area that should be handled with a sensitivity that always has the healing of the family as the responsibility. Children mature at different rates, and to assume that they are mature enough to handle the details of infidelity is a mistake. While parents need to take responsibility for the failure of their marriage, the details should not be shared with them. The language that should be used is "Mommy did something that has hurt Daddy, and we are trying to fix it" or "Daddy did something that he is not proud of, and he is sorry that it has hurt the family." I am not suggesting that parents ignore the need for children to have answers. Still, I am asking that we remember they are young and that parents with sensitivity should examine the level of information provided for them. We must guard the welfare and emotional stability of the next generation. Parents' ultimate goal should be to help children matriculate through the journey and reality of divorce with the least lasting emotional impact.

As parents, we must never forget that our primary responsibility is teaching the next generation. During divorce, we can reinforce many character traits as we model how to handle pain, disappointment, and strength in times of stress. Children are more observant than we often give them credit for. As we navigate the divorce journey and begin new relationships, we must remain keenly aware that we are still teaching our children. Parents must carefully introduce new relationships and individuals into their children's lives. Without sounding overtly spiritual, I must remind parents that you remain married until your divorce is final. Introducing external relationships before the divorce is finalized models' behavior that teaches children not to honor vows and covenants. While I ultimately believe that divorce is not the perfect will of God, there are times when divorce is the necessary reality of the hardness of the heart and the breach of covenant. It does, however, remain very important that we model the correct behavior even as we work towards the finality of our marital relationship. Introducing new relationships must be handled with genuine sensitivity. As you explore new personal relationships, initially be very discreet about them. We teach our children through our behavior. Your child should not be introduced to every person you date. During this time, children must be reassured that they are not being displaced and that the other parent is not being replaced. Also, the reality of a new relationship could negatively trigger your child's hope for parental reconciliation, which can lead to a feeling of animosity. Don't have unrealistic expectations regarding how your child will respond to the new relationship. Remember that your child is a child. Communicate your desire for how they will embrace the new relationship. What should your new significant other be called? What are the relational expectations when both parents are together for special days? It is much easier to be proactive in this season than reactive.

One of the most tragic ways to handle these new relationships is by surprise. Springing new relationships on our children can cause lasting difficulties that challenge developing a genuine connection. I often suggest that when one parent has begun a new relationship after divorce, the news should be shared with the other parent first as a common courtesy. It must be noted that this only works when the parents have agreed to be civil towards one another. Often, the unresolved baggage prevents parents from establishing healthy relationship parameters that only hurt the children. When parents can process their pain effectively, it creates an environment that allows the communication between parents to remain open and productive. After communicating that one of the parents is beginning to establish a new relationship, the plan for introducing the individual to the children can be discussed. It is unfair to prevent the child from developing a relationship with the new individual. However, the mistake is introducing a new relationship too soon. It is confusing to children when we introduce them to multiple relationships. Children should only be introduced to relationships that have become serious. When my wife Valerie and I began dating, she did not allow me to come to her home or meet her son (our son) until our relationship reached a level of seriousness where we were moving toward marriage. The time of parental dating serves as a tremendous opportunity to model and teach our children about relationships and dating. Introducing new relationships to your children too early, before the relationship is fully vested, can display a behavior that is not typically healthy for developing sound relationship principles in the next generation.

Also, when going through a divorce, both parents must commit to spending as much time with the children as possible. This is a vulnerable time for young people; try not to over-promise and work diligently to keep promises made. It is only natural that the new living arrangements will create conditions for one parent to become closer to the child. Even in situations where custody is shared, it is virtually impossible to maintain equity in a relationship. You cannot cut the child in half, and time cannot be fully equally shared. Do not pressure the children or make them feel guilty for the affection displayed to one of the parents. They need you both, and this is, unfortunately, a result of the decision to divorce.

It also becomes important to recognize and validate the feelings of young people. Allow them to express their emotions. Observe changes in behavior that could point to unresolved anger and unchecked feelings. Permit them to be upset, but also establish a program for properly addressing their resentment. One of the greatest needs during this time for a child is consistency. To the best of the parents' ability, plan the week and recalibrate family traditions such as Christmas and birthdays. As difficult as divorce is, it can become an opportunity to create an atmosphere of mutual respect if the parents commit to planning and communication.

Finally, always work to be amicable. Children are very intelligent and can pick up or perceive when there is tension between parents. Work through that tension as much as possible before being in their presence. Children should not be penalized for the decisions of adults. Communicating with your child's school and teacher about what is happening is also extremely helpful. This gives the teacher important insight into any potential behavior changes and helps to reinforce the added sensitivity that your child might require while navigating this difficult season.

"Children spell love... T-I-M-E."

- Dr. A. Witham

A Kingdom Parenting Approach
to Healing Generations and Transforming Legacies

Children And Relationships

I have seen parents introducing concepts of dating that children are too young to comprehend. We do it light-heartedly when they are very small by referring to other children as their girlfriends or boyfriends. Although these moments seem harmless and innocent in kindergarten or elementary school, we can never forget that children learn and grow at a different pace than when we were young. One of the chief challenges I see in parenting today is the failure to allow children to be children. We often introduce children to concepts of life that are too mature. Allow little girls to play with their dolls and be little girls. Allow little boys to play cowboys and soldiers. As our children mature, we must also remain careful about introducing them to dating concepts. As a parent, your child's first date should always be with you. A father should be the first date for his daughter, and a mother should be the first date for her son. This concept is a practical teaching opportunity. The main objective is to teach young people personal self-esteem and the core values of dating. Mothers should show their sons how to respond to a young lady on a date. Holding the door, allowing her to order first at dinner, and walking next to the curb on the sidewalk are all concepts of chivalry that must be taught to our sons. While the lessons are not limited to just these, they are a great starting point. Fathers should teach their daughters to expect this respect from a date. As stated earlier, parents should be our children's paramount teachers and models of behavior.

We also fail to communicate valuable and transparent truth to our children. Equipping our children with the truth about real-life issues prepares them to make good decisions and understand the consequences of their decisions. Children must be clear on their parent's expectations. Other related areas of concern are being clear on the age to begin dating and wearing makeup. Whenever I dedicate a baby, I pray that the parents will not fall victim to sociological peer pressure as the stewards of their child's life. I will not suggest a specific age for young girls to wear makeup or the age your child should date. But I will remind parents that we permit our children to grow up too fast. While I understand the need for little girls to play dress up and play in their moms' makeup, it is still different to allow them to wear makeup. Not only does it have the potential to damage their skin, but it can also damage their self-esteem. I must also remind every parent that you must model what you are attempting to teach. Mothers who dress provocatively will find it difficult to teach their daughters to dress conservatively. As a child, I could never pressure my mother into compromising her standards. I would remind her what other parents were allowing their children to do to no avail. She always responded, "I have nothing to do with how they run their house. This is my house." We must be committed to establishing our standards. Standards of curfew and standards of behavior. Be clear about the qualifications and timing of rites of passage, like wearing makeup, dating, and attending more mature social moments. Another way I see today's parents assisting our children in growing up fast is in styling. My daughter still talks about how I would not allow her mother to fix her hair in adult styles until she had reached a certain age. When she was a little girl, I wanted her to wear ponytails. Moms don't kill the messenger when you hear the next message. My daughter did not get perms in her hair at a very young age. She wore ponytails with a bang in the front. I wanted her to look like a little girl, not a grown woman. While all circumstances are different, many mothers tell me they put relaxers in their daughter's hair because it is easier for them. While it might be easier, stop to remember what it is doing to her hair. The same can be said about weaves and other types of hairstyles like braids that are very heavy and can have long-term effects on the child's real hair and scalp. Children grow up fast enough without parents accelerating the process.

Our sons are being judged and treated in ways that can break their spirit. As a parent of a male child, I often found it challenging to provide guidance without sounding overbearing. I hope we create an atmosphere of education and guidance that teaches our young men real-life lessons before they learn them the hard way. One of the realities of many parents is that we operate with a do as I say because I said it mentality rather than taking the time to explain our perspective. Remind young people of how the structure of our society has many unwritten rules that can add additional barriers to success. Especially with young men, there are many sociological hindrances to success. I attempted to empower my son with real-life evidence about growing up as a black man and how his decisions about his circle and his appearance were important. One of his most significant responses to me during this season was, "I am not worried about what people think." While I applauded his mental independence and self-confidence, I also made it clear that he would be judged first by his race, then his appearance, and finally, his circle. While I am saddened that young men have to be so sensitive to the oppressive sociological realities of our day, it is essential that we, as parents, explain all the rules of the sociological game that we are playing. Parents with sons should teach them how to handle being stopped by the police. Teach them how to make good relationship choices. Please help them to understand that they are making life decisions daily.

As we commit to providing our children with the resources to become productive in how they handle relationships, one of the areas that require sensitivity is sibling relationships. Much family dysfunction among adult siblings can be traced to parental influences when they were children. Let me point out different social-family conditions we must be sensitive to. The gender composition of children in families includes a boy being raised with sisters or a girl being raised with multiple brothers but no sisters. Human nature tells us that fathers are usually harder on sons than daughters. At the same time, mothers can be harder on daughters than sons. Add to this reality that every child is unique, and the first child is usually held to a higher standard than the children born later. Parents must always remain aware of sibling dynamics in the family. Understanding that older children are usually bossy, middle children can have identity trouble, and the youngest child can become selfish, it becomes the parent's responsibility to create and cultivate an atmosphere in the home committed to ensuring each child develops productively and positively. Considering these realities, parents must also study each child individually and become sensitive to the personality traits of each child. Understanding which children are more introverted or extroverted and their other personality traits enables parents to understand how to administer discipline, be a source of encouragement, and ultimately, how to read each child as an individual. A parent who remains aware of the children's differences, personalities, and giftings will be a tremendous source of inspiration and guidance in the life of their children.

I am a firm believer that racism is a taught character trait. Children are not born racist. It is alarming to see the level of division in our society currently. While I am aware that we are a product of the context and dispensation of time in which we are raised, many people are simply a product of hatred. I am godly proud of my grandchildren and their ability to see beyond race in choosing and building their social relationships; I am fully aware that much of the credit for their racial openness is a product of their parents. As parents, I think two major concepts must be taught to our children about racism. First, our children must be taught the history and reality of racism. Parents are afraid to address the big elephant in society, which is the fact that racism exists. To ignore the reality of racism simply adds to the reality of it. Regardless of your ethnicity, it becomes the responsibility of parents to address it. Be clear with your children that racism is not to be tolerated in any way. Bigotry is a deadly character trait in all shapes. We must teach our children that all of humanity is God's creation, and that God loves every person. While I might not agree with the standards that everyone desires to live by, I must respect everyone. Teaching our children to respect everyone, even those with whom we have spiritual, social, or political differences, is vital. Not only must we teach our children to accept all people, but we must teach them not to be silent when they observe bigotry or injustice. Silence is a form of approval. Teach your children the truth about racism and make clear your standards and expectations. Instructing our children about the reality of racism prepares them to address it when confronted with it. Point out racism when seen so that young people will be clear on how to identify it. Perhaps many people will disagree with me and feel that we should not spend time and effort teaching our children about the history and reality of racism, but I disagree. To negate teaching our children about racism is to leave them confused and ignorant. Our children must be equipped to operate relationally in our society, and this education prepares them to accept and respect all people while confronting these ills of our society and culture. Please know that racists are teaching their children, bigots are teaching their children, and we must teach our children if we are ever to overcome the hatred and division of this day. We should desire well-rounded children who become social agents of change and unity. This can only happen when we become proactive in their development in and outside the home. If we teach our children, we strike a blow against the influences of the world that will most definitely be working hard to have a negative impact on their future.

"Children grieve deeply, yet their little hearts possess an incredible resilience. It's our duty to be their pillars of support, helping them process loss with honesty, patience, and the unwavering assurance that, even in the darkest moments, love remains a guiding light."

- Anonymous

Children And Death

Death is unavoidable, and guiding our children through the loss of a loved one is crucial for their future mental well-being and ability to handle trauma. Assisting children in dealing with grief is one of the most sensitive responsibilities of a parent. Often, parents fail to remember that children don't always have the emotional fortitude to deal with the stress of death and grieving and, most times, need additional professional support to overcome the burden of losing a close relationship. When talking to children about dying, death, and grief, make a genuine attempt to use simple words that express their concerns with clarity. At the beginning of the grieving process, it is imperative to be a committed listener and to provide a safe space for comfort and sharing. This is a time to express expectations and what the future will look like. Children need to know and have a sense of stability.

I have often found that when a loved one has died, the adults convene to a space of decision-making and then report to the younger generation what will happen. While I understand that children should not be the primary decision-makers, allowing them to be a part of some of the decisions is central. Asking a child what Grandma would want can be a source of validation and healing. Also, providing an opportunity for them to reflect and remember their loved one assists in bringing closure and gives value to their relationship with the deceased. Explaining events such as funerals, burials, and other related components of celebrating acknowledges your child's special relationship with the loved one who has died. Almost every time I deal with a family in death, someone says, "We must be strong; Mom would not want us crying," or "I have to be strong for my children." While I understand the desire to display strength, I have also become keenly aware that allowing children to see us grieve permits them to grieve. Many young people have never been allowed to grieve properly, which can cause complications in other areas of their life and maturation.

We must also be aware of how children process death based on age. Children are naturally curious, so be prepared to be confronted with serious questions about death by natural causes or suicide, burials, cremations, heaven, and, yes, even hell. A loved one who dies suddenly and unexpectedly poses different questions than one who becomes sick and progressively moves toward death. Every situation is different and should be handled independently. Be patient as young people process and give them time to grieve at their rate of healing. I often suggest that after talking to a child about death, you have a preplanned activity or topic that helps your child feel a little better.

When children are very young, they often worry about their health, or the health of others close to them. Reassure them you are fine, and so are they. Closely monitor behavior and attitudes to diagnose their grief process properly. The decision about whether a child should attend a funeral should be made on a case-by-case basis. It is essential to create an opportunity for them to view their loved one; perhaps the funeral is not the best place or time for that moment. Private moments are always helpful in providing an atmosphere to inspire a healthy and productive grief process.

The process of grieving should always attempt to accomplish several things. First, the acceptance of the reality that a loved one has died. Next, develop methods that provide the opportunity to properly process the emotional upheaval death creates. It is essential as well to assist the child in adjusting to life without the deceased. Become sensitive to the date on which loved ones passed and use their memory as a platform to celebrate that life. Be extra aware of national days of celebration and how they may have an impact. Father's Day, Mother's Day, Christmas, and Thanksgiving can all resurface memories that can plunge someone into depression. Finally, providing an emotional connection point is vital. Assist them in celebrating and remembering personal moments particular to their relationship. The more memories you can sacredly and truthfully offer, the more potentially stable a young person will be as they matriculate through grief. Most psychologists call this the three R's of processing grief: recognition, remembering, and rebuilding. Some suggest that children should not attend funerals. In contrast, I have learned to recognize that each situation is different while understanding that funerals reinforce the reality of death.

My wife and I usually process our emotions differently. This has taught a valuable lesson about how people process their emotions. Remember that each child is different and will process their grief differently. When observing your child, remember to reflect on each child's personality. Some will cry, others will be withdrawn, while others might display anger. Giving each child the opportunity to grieve independently while providing close observation is very important.

Children tend to process through five stages of grief. These stages are denial, anger, bargaining, depression, and acceptance. Bargaining is usually one of the most difficult stages for adults to handle. In this stage, children will often attempt to make a promise to God or other authorities in exchange for returning their loved ones. This is a normal stage and should not overwhelm parents but become a source of information about the overall grief process. Each stage can operate independently, and there are no time constraints for each step, as parents observe and evaluate whether progress is being made. In young people, grief can come in waves; at times, it takes as much as 18 months to see the expected improvement and evidence of definitive healing. It is not unusual to notice changes such as sleep patterns, loss of appetite, or social isolation during this time.

Children: Authority And Fellowship

We live in a social atmosphere where respect for authority has declined into an unhealthy reality. When I first began pastoring, there was a significant respect for ministers, teachers, police officers, civic leaders, and those who hold leadership roles in our community. While I will readily admit that the loss of respect has grown out of the reality that many in positions of authority have breached the accountability of their leadership role. However, the parents are responsible for teaching and instilling respect for authority in their children. Growing up, the teacher was right until proven wrong. If I came home with a note from the teacher, it was a felony, not a misdemeanor. As parents, we must always teach our children best through our model. How do you respond when addressing police officers? What do our children hear us saying about our boss' and the work environment? What behavior do we display when engaging co-workers? Whenever I see a parent responding negatively to an educator or school administrator in front of their children, I think about how the next generation will respond. I have discovered that the seeds of our actions mature more definitively in each generation. Let me explain. Have you ever noticed that every generation appears stronger and more capable than the previous generation? That means that modeling bad behavior is like a seed planted that will grow larger in the next generation. I still remember going to work with my mother and observing how she responded to her boss. They were not friends. They were boss and subordinate. I have already said this, but it is worth repeating. More is caught than taught. Displaying respect for authority in front of our children is a must. This also includes teaching our children how to respond in difficult times and with difficult people. At home, practice acting out different scenarios. Especially with the social division in which we live, it is vital to ensure that our children know proper responses in moments like engaging the police. Teach our young males how to respond when pulled over. Remember that if we are not teaching them, social media is! One of the things my wife did when our children were teenagers was to remind them every time, they left the house. We learn what we repeat! It breaks my heart to hear a child say, "My momma is coming up here to show out today." We are developing a next-generation show-out mentality. It is also important to remember that we can teach our children how to respect authority even when we disagree with it. I am not suggesting blind obedience; I am advocating we become instructors in communicating and responding to authority in all situations. We can communicate our concerns without being disrespectful. And we can also display behavior and teach respect for authority when we are disrespected. I remember deciding to eat in a small-town restaurant known for displaying racism. On this particular day, I was handling business in the city. I did not have a choice to eat in a more racially sensitive location. I had my son LJay with me. We sat down, and it took quite some time for someone to come over and greet us to take our order. It was clear that they desired for us to eat somewhere else. The waitress continued to socialize with other patrons. She deliberately served us in a manner that communicated that we were not a priority. After eating our meal and paying for our tab, I left the waitress a significant tip. When we got in the car, my son asked me why I had tipped the lady when her service was terrible. I used the situation as a teachable moment for my son. I reminded him that the best way to respond to racism was to let her see a black man honor her despite her disrespectful behavior. Never underestimate the power of simple moments that become classrooms for life lessons.

When I was young, one of the lessons I remember from my parents and grandparents was their respect for custodians. My mother would always speak to them when passing while they were accomplishing their daily assignments. As a boy, I remember walking through a freshly mopped floor in the hospital and my mother making me apologize to the custodian for tracking dirt on his floor. Can I tell you that even today, I always greet a custodian and never walk through their freshly mopped floor? In a school environment, the custodian is in a place of authority, just like any other adult.

I am not just preaching about the good old days. Still, I champion a mentality of training children to be sensitive to adult authority. Would you permit me to hypothesize that perhaps one of the most significant ways we have contributed to the erosion of respect from generation to generation is by giving an audience to young people too early? When I was a boy growing up, I was not allowed to be present and participate in adult conversations.

Allowing young people to be present in these moments gives them a sense of social equality. As I write, I hear my mother's voice sharing, "This is grown folks' business," as she instructs me to leave the room. Parents are forcing and enabling their children to grow up too fast by allowing them to be present and participate in adult conversations. This fosters an environment that causes them to think they are adults and, therefore, lose respect for adult authority. As a pastor, I have seen this aggravate our society as the institution of marriage has eroded. Many times, parents who are wounded and feel isolated in their relationship trauma begin to vent to their children, causing children to begin to feel like they are adults. One of the most defined moments in my childhood was when I called an adult by their first name. My mother made it clear it was never appropriate for me to address any adult by their first name. Even today, I still address my elders or those in authority as Mr. or Mrs. As simple as it may sound, allowing children to refer to adults by their first name is inspiring a sense of lack of respect. As parents, we must remind ourselves that our children are not our friends or equals. They are our generational project. We are stewards of their destiny. We are their chief instructors. We are their first line of training and development. In everything we display, our children learn lessons that will either propel or hinder them.

Children And Community

Our children must learn to navigate all types of relationships to have a successful life. Paternal and maternal relationships in the family. Social relationships in school and friends. But little is ever said about the social relationships of the community. I have seen the erosion of respect for extended community relationships. I am sure you have heard the statement, "It takes a village to raise a child." That is correct, but for the village to be a part of our children's lives, we must teach them how to respect the community in their village. Years ago, I started to give bicycles away at Christmas as a way of serving our community. When we first began, parents would require their children to go home and write thank you letters to our church expressing their gratitude for the act of kindness. I then observed how few young people would write a thank you note year after year. Then, children would not say thank you when receiving the gift of a new bicycle. We even had children complain about the color of the free bicycle they received. This reality is evidence of the social erosion in how we train our children to operate in life. Parents, we have to make sure that we train our children to be sensitive to the civic responsibility of improving their context and respecting those who are poor in their lives. We have created a generation of young people who feel entitled. Maybe they have been watching their parents! No one owes you anything. My mother always told me, "People do not have to be kind to you." We must teach our children to appreciate and cultivate civic and community relationships. As simple as it may sound, it is about displaying respect for people. When your child receives a new bicycle, it becomes an insult when they say to the giver, "I don't want a blue bicycle." Unfortunately, I must lay much of the blame at the feet of parents. Do you remember when children brought their teacher gifts on special days? Instead of gifts, parents curse teachers, and children are insubordinate in the classroom. Not to preach, but the Bible says, "A gift makes room for us." It is not about abilities but about an expression of sacrifice and gratitude. It is vitally important for parents to become more sensitive to training children on how to be socially responsible in the civic community. It can be as simple as requiring your child to call someone on the phone to express their appreciation. We must begin to retrain a generation of entitled young people. We created this monster, and we must reign it in. Perhaps one of the paramount reasons parents need to consider redirecting this behavior is because everyone will eventually need someone. You cannot survive in a social vacuum.

When we were children, everyone in the neighborhood or on your block was part of a big extended family. Now, we live in such selfie-sensitive realities that we don't even know our neighbor's names. We have to model for our children being community service and empowerment aware. We no longer help our neighbors in times of trouble. One generation ago, if a neighbor was sick or supporting a sick family member, we cooked for them, served them, cut their grass, and pulled in their trash cans. We must return to this type of community. Life cannot revolve around you and your family only. How does your family affect the community or neighborhood in which you live? Is your apartment building or condo complex better because of your family's existence? Do your children have a sense of empathy for others? This behavior must be modeled and prioritized if our children become more aware of the need to have civic and community impact. Our communities will only be as strong as the families that are a part of the composition of the community itself. I recently witnessed my daughter writing thank you cards to everyone in our village who gave her and her husband a gift as they expected their first child. She grew up observing her mother write thank you cards when people would give to us. I have discovered that when we become productive adults, we can look at our lives and note how, at every turn and transition of life, someone helped us survive and succeed. While we cannot fully control the community we are raised in, we can adjust and affect how we develop and respond to it as we grow and matriculate through the seasons of life.

Whenever our community is in crisis, we can model and teach our children how to develop a desire to impact our community. When there is a community tragedy, lead your children to participate in community healing. Let them see you giving, sharing, and participating in community and civic service moments. Don't just read about the bad news near you; sit down with your children and discuss the current situations, problems, and community dynamics. Express your concerns and help them process their mental and emotional issues. Allow them to ask questions and be honest with your responses. Point out the difficult social concerns in your community and help them to shape and form their social ideology. The only way we will solve much of the social ills of our day is to raise a generation that thinks independently and embraces the assignment of positively impacting the community in which they live. I believe our children can restore the character of our society. Still, they need the guidance of previous generations as anchors of stability, instruction, and social compassion.

"Embrace change, for under new management, the seeds of innovation are sown, and the promise of a brighter future unfolds."

-Anonymous

Under New Management

In the book of Joshua, one of the most significant verses is 24:15, where the patriarch makes a declaration that has enduring implications for his family. Joshua declares, "Choose you this day whom you will serve, but as for me and my house, we will serve the Lord." The backdrop of this scriptural declaration very closely resembles the times we live in. The standards of society were eroding, and the social pressure to conform to living contrary to the covenant principles of Jehovah was becoming evident in every component of their community. In the modern-day vernacular, Joshua makes a statement to his family and the community; essentially, he says, "No more boiling of our children! This family is under new management." As you have read this book, I want you to reach a place of declaration, just like Joshua. Today is your day of reckoning. It is where the proverbial rubber hits the road. Stand up to the adversary, the social pressures, and your insecurities and declare that your family is under new management. Decide to allow Jehovah to be the guiding force in how your family and household operate. Gather the kids and the dog, have a family meeting, and establish a new baseline for the next generation. Don't waiver; you can do this. Before it is too late, snatch your family away from the enemy. You might be asking, "How do I do it?" I'm glad you asked. There are several things that this new season will require.

The first thing you will need to do is display sanctification. As the parent, you must accept the leadership role of ensuring that the spirituality standard is modeled in your home. As parents, our children must see us praying, worshipping, and seeing God as a priority. Joshua begins his declaration in Chapter 24, verse 15, with the word "me." You must enter an "as for me" season. As a parent, stop and do some personal reflection, and honestly evaluate your relationship with Christ. The spiritual movement and maturity of your family begin with you. Parents are the standard bearers for the spiritual growth of their children. Your children will mirror your behavior and pursue God when they see you pursue God.

Secondly, as parents, you must define standards for the family. Joshua fully declares that "we will serve the Lord." I often see serving parents who inspire their children to serve in the kingdom create an atmosphere for spiritual formation in the children. Search for opportunities to serve the kingdom that include your family serving. Feeding the homeless, working in the local church, and volunteering in the community instill in your children an awareness to be agents of service. In many churches, there are opportunities to serve together. I am always blessed to see a father and son giving out turkeys at Thanksgiving. You have heard the proverb that a family that prays together stays together. I believe a family that serves together grows together. Serving reminds us how blessed we are. When we lead our children in serving, we create an atmosphere of gratitude and appreciation. Most of our children live in a shelter of ignorance of the true social ills and dilemmas. Serving develops an attitude of compassion and creates a sensitivity to other people's needs.

Next, if you are going to create and cultivate this new family consciousness as a parent, you must develop socialization. In the same chapter of Joshua, it is made clear that everyone will not and does not decide to follow Jehovah. Have you noticed that the current generation of young people lacks social skills? They do not know how to disagree. They have learned how to handle conflict from what they see and hear from social media. They lack independent thinking skills and often fall victim to conformity. They end arguments with gunfire. They develop relationships with people that are unhealthy for their destiny. Not to insult you, but this also sounds like many adults. Joshua makes it clear that everyone will not choose to live in a Godly covenant. It is as if he is attempting to teach his household about living in the world but not living by the concepts and standards of the world. We must help our children to understand how to respect everyone but not agree with everyone. We are accountable to help them develop social skills. Teach them how to handle difficult people. Show them how to respect different people. Model how to be in a relationship with those they disagree with without becoming disagreeable.

Finally, as a parent genuinely attempting to take control of your family's spiritual growth and development in the agent of change that God desires, you must demonstrate salvation. Begin to think generationally. As a parent, assume the responsibility of generations. Everything you do to inspire and develop your family today has a generational impact. Your children will eventually become parents. Joshua declares, "As for me and my family." Family is more than just what you see today. The Bible talks about how God deals with us spiritually for at least four generations. I once heard Steve Harvey say that he was working so that his great-great-grandchildren, who might never know him, would have to acknowledge his impact on their family. That is the pentacle of our parental assignment. We are responsible for shaping generations, not a generation. We are breaking the generational curse and creating generational blessings. As for me and my "family." Family does not end with those who live in your home. Family is your bloodline. Protect the assignment on your bloodline. You are the one God has called to ensure the spiritual victory of your children, grandchildren, and their children. You have been equipped for this assignment. Hopefully, this book has been used by God as a resource to empower you, inspire you, and motivate you to reclaim and restore the order of your home. Put the sign in the window today: "Under New Management."

*A Kingdom Parenting Approach
to Healing Generations and Transforming Legacies*

"I call Heaven and Earth to witness against you today; I place before you Life and Death, Blessing and Curse. Choose life so that you and your children will live."

-Deuteronomy 30:19

The Choice Is Yours

We have reached the end of our journey towards establishing a kingdom-minded family. As a quick recap, every problem in our society can be traced back to the breakdown of the nuclear family. The family was never meant to be perfect, but it was created to establish an order on earth. If our society is to ever establish respect for people we are tasked to operate relationally and become the training ground for future generations. We must commit to creating family structures that enable and empower our children.

Rahab saved her entire family by changing her behavior. The irony of Rahab's story was that she was far from perfect yet became the family savior. Each of us is a product of the decisions we make daily. Every failure and every success are a product of our decisions. Decisions about relationships, associations, careers, finance, etc. The good news is that it is not too late, despite where you are today. Whether married, single, or divorced, today is the day to choose. Today is your day to decide how your family's future will unfold. This is a crossroads of family destiny. What will be the legacy of your family? What will your family's name mean 40, 60, 100 years from now? Will your family make a mark and leave a mark that will never be erased? If you answer yes, let's finish what we started in chapter one.

Suppose you are a parent committed to securing your family's future and ensuring that your family's destiny is fulfilled. In that case, you must begin to do intentional modeling. I have discovered that we have daily opportunities for instruction on how we handle the person cutting us off in traffic. How do we respond to the unprofessional clerk in the store? What we say about co-workers, neighbors, or family members at the dinner table matters. The everyday stresses of life are all opportunities to teach our children. Never forget much more is caught than taught. The old saying "do what I say and not what I do" is outdated. Our children are going to do what they see us do. We are the premier example in their lives. Train yourself to remember I'm being watched. At times, I find it amusing, and at other times, disappointing when I see my children model exactly what I have displayed. Racist parents model racism. Arguing parents model a difficulty in compromise. Gossiping is not a natural reflex; it results from gossiping parents. We transfer our patterns of behavior by how we carry ourselves daily. Whatever we display becomes the acceptable behavior for our children.

As we decide to make choices that empower our family, we must also be careful to inspire ministry. Before you get confused, please let me explain. I believe that everyone has a ministry to fulfill. No, I am not saying everyone is a pastor or a preacher. But everyone has an assignment and a responsibility to leave every context we are engaged in better than before we arrived. Our children must see our social consciousness as we participate in our daily responsibilities. Teach them to be sensitive to people experiencing homelessness. Let the ladies get off the elevator first. We need to model looking for opportunities to serve, not just in church but in the community. Join the PTA at your child's school. Show the teachers, custodians, and bus drivers respect and appreciation. One of the things I remember as a child is my mom giving the mailman a Christmas gift. Unfortunately, we have become masters at teaching our children to chase a dollar, compete with social media images, and look out for themselves above others. Ministry simply means serving. Teach your children how to serve. Help them look for ways to serve their community. These are simply suggestions; the point is that we must inspire a behavior of service and sensitivity for others.

We live in a society where falling into the comparison trap becomes easy. Most young people who go contrary to a productive destiny are not bad children. Most children with whom I have had to go to court were good young people with bright futures. Well, then, what led to them astray? You will be astounded by my answer. The simple truth is they became followers rather than leaders. We must train our children to be leaders and not followers. How do we do that? We do this by becoming people who live by the concept of independent management. In Joshua chapter 24, Joshua declares you choose how your family will live and operate. Still, as for my family, "we will" serve the Lord. We have got to become a *we will* generation. As parents, we cannot continue to compromise our standards of behavior. Our children need to know what our standards are, what we believe, and what our core beliefs are. My children were taught we respect everyone. Everyone has value.

We have to help young people to have confidence in who they are. One of the ways we do this at a very young age is by celebrating their growth and accomplishments. I'm not talking about providing participation trophies but acknowledging them positively when they display behavior that reinforces our values and core beliefs. Our family believes in the value and importance of education. My young grandson has never had a haircut. No, he is not a Nazarite. His hair is naturally curly and has allowed us to reinforce his individuality. My daughter-in-love has assisted him in writing a book entitled, "My Curls Are My Confidence." Recently, he had a book signing in the park. This moment has accomplished at least two things. It has reinforced his confidence in his individuality and raised funds for his academic future. We can inspire our children to believe in themselves, remain committed to their core values and standards, and constantly remind them that they are leaders, not followers. In that case, we will successfully raise the next generation of change agents. Parents celebrate their individuality, cultivate their leadership, and celebrate their victories and progress. Unfortunately, as parents, most communication is correcting rather than celebrating. We can also create a culture of confidence by celebrating them regularly. Constantly correcting behavior and illuminating failures can risk causing a child to grow up with low self-value and low confidence. Yes, we must correct behavioral challenges and ensure that young people know our expectations. However, there must be a balance between correction and celebration. One of the most eye-opening statements from my son was when he communicated that I sometimes make him feel like he never gets anything right —hearing him make that statement pierced me to my core. It forced me to self-examine and become much more sensitive to letting him know when I am proud of him. If your child would share with you, would they feel the same?

I have discovered that it is not enough to simply raise productive children. I want to raise children that have an influencing mentality. I truly believe our assignment is to raise game-changers. Whatever space we enter should be transformed by our presence. After Joshua declared how his family would operate, the people replied, "We would never abandon the Lord and serve other gods." I am constantly reminding my children that we are chosen to influence. I am proud of how my children have influenced their particular circles of relationship. I believe everyone I come into contact with should think differently after spending time with me. We are called to be salt and light, as both serve as sources of influence. They share the ability to influence the atmosphere. Wherever I work, go to school, or simply socialize will be different because of my presence. My family does not attempt to be a source of influence because we are in ministry but because that is a family assignment. Influence births responsibility. We must assist our children in understanding their responsibility to create and cultivate the atmosphere in which we desire. This influence must be more than simply a spiritual reality. We have the responsibility to be spiritual, cultural, and sociological influencers. One of the most significant ways we become influencers is by speaking up and being vocal. Teaching our children not to be silent when they observe injustices is very important. We can train our children to be influencers in many ways.

Make sure that your child understands their particular gifts and abilities. Never forget that family and friends are the two biggest influencers in your child's life. Current surveys say that 86% of young Americans desire to be influencers on social media. I'm not necessarily talking about that type of influence. By definition (Merriam-Webster), the word means to have the power of producing an effect without apparent exertion of force or direct exercise of command. Confident people tend to become influencers in whatever environment they operate. Enabling them to identify moments in which their influence was obvious is also important.

I believe you are either the influencer or you are being influenced. Ask your child about their friends. Be honest about your opinions of your child's friends and explain why you feel like you do. Point out moments when your child is a follower rather than a leader. Do this often; don't grow weary in well doing. As parents, our children need us daily, especially in moments of failure. Helping a child navigate times of failure develops resilience. Everyone fails. I guess I need to quote my wife, Valerie. She reminds our children that we never fail; we have teaching moments. Help young people to deal positively with moments of disappointment and disaster. This will maintain and develop confidence.

We can also assist our children by reminding them that they are leaders, too. Surround your children with them. We can accomplish this by enrolling them in camps, giving them volunteer opportunities at churches, teaching them communication skills, and, above all, encouraging them never to quit. One of the most significant detriments to becoming a source of influence is quitting. Quitting erodes confidence a little at a time. I told our children we finish what we start in spite of the struggle. A simple way to build a child's confidence is to provide teaching moments in the house for your child. Maybe once a week, have your child prepare and teach a lesson on a subject to the family; this builds confidence, enhances communication skills, and develops leadership while expanding your child's intellect. Give children the time and responsibility to fix their problems. Too many parents work hard to keep their children from disappointment, so they bail them out and short-circuit their leadership growth. When possible, allow children to make their own decisions so they may learn the reality of consequences. Encourage your child to look for leadership opportunities, like serving on school committees. I know you think that will add work to you as a parent; that is what parenting is! Finally, I believe children suffer from a lack of exposure. We must develop opportunities to expose our children to more than they see. A large percentage of children have never traveled outside their context. The most significant benefit of traveling is creating a culture of dreaming. Today, my children travel the world because they were exposed to it at an early age. Travel inspires, educates, and expands perspectives. When our children were young, they were happy to speak up in class about places we had gone that was part of their lesson. They were proud to have visited the USS Arizona Memorial, a part of Pearl Harbor in Hawaii. When we travel, we should have the objective of teaching and bonding. When our children were young, we allowed them to bring a friend with us on vacation. When they became adults, they informed me that our simple act of inviting their friends taught them to be open and giving to others. Little did they know that our thinking was to bring them a playmate or friend, so we did not have to work so hard. One of the most impactful moments about vacation planning is deciding where to go. Although both of our children are grown, we still take a family vacation every year that includes the families of my children's spouses. Last and most importantly, travel models the importance of family time. It is not as important to where you go; it is about the time together, not the destination. So, get those passports and travel the world, making more memories along the way.

A Kingdom Parenting Approach
to Healing Generations and Transforming Legacies

A Final Prayer

God our Father, as the parent of
(say the names of your children aloud),
I come to you today asking that you provide me with the wisdom to steward their lives.
Thank you for trusting me with the assignment of training this child to become the leader you have called them to be.
Give me the discernment to know when and how to provide discipline and guidance.
I ask for patience as I attempt to be the parent that you have called me to be.
I pray for angels of protection to cover my child daily.
I pray for their potential to be manifested and declare that my child is a world changer.
I pray for provision to be able to supply the needs of my child and declare that every need in my child's life is already taken care of.

A Kingdom Parenting Approach
to Healing Generations and Transforming Legacies

Please guard my child from any unhealthy influences and bring those people who are connected to my child's future into their social circle.

I stand against all works of the adversary planned to derail my child's destiny.

I believe that my child was created with a particular purpose on earth.

My child shall live to do profound things and have a kingdom global impact in Jesus' name.

~~~~

I trust I have assisted in equipping you with the mental, relational, and parental tools needed to take your family to another level. Together, we can turn off the stove and begin to commit to stop *Boiling Our Children*!

A Kingdom Parenting Approach
to Healing Generations and Transforming Legacies

Additional Book Titles

To purchase please visit: www.KWBrownMinistries.org

Marriage Talk:
Cultivating a Successful Marriage
Through Self-Examination
Bishop Kim W. Brown

What's In A Title
A New Leadership Paradigm
Dr. Valerie K. Brown

The Miseducation of the Christian
Dr. Valerie K. Brown

You Can't Do What?
The Real Meaning of Your Salvation
Dr. Valerie K. Brown

Creating Pastures
A Plan for Kingdom Legacy
for the Church and Family
Bishop Kim W. Brown
Dr. Valerie K. Brown

www.ingramcontent.com/pod-product-compliance
Lightning Source LLC
LaVergne TN
LVHW010330070526
838199LV00065B/5705